When I'm With You

Dedication

For Ashley,
a faithful reader and sweet friend
I am blessed to know you

You have made known to me the path of life;
you will fill me with joy in your presence,
with eternal pleasures at your right hand.

Psalm 16:11

Chapter One

Amber entered the college dorm room and felt incredibly tired. They had been on the road since eight a.m., and now it was almost eight o'clock in the evening. She had been excited when they left from Seth's house this morning on the sunny, late-summer day, feeling ready to take this new path in her life. But now she felt dead. The air-conditioning had gone out in the car, and it had been hot today.

Traveling into the northern California mountains had provided some relief, along with the stop along the beach before having dinner. But they had run into road construction during the remaining distance to the school. They should have been here at least an hour ago, and Amber felt ready for bed, but she had some unpacking to do first.

Seth carried her two suitcases into the room and set them beside the bed. She lowered the bag from her shoulder along with another one in her hands and laid her pillow on the bare mattress. Her sheets were in one of her suitcases, but her quilt and other blanket were still in the car.

Amber heard Kerri come in behind them and take her things to the other side of the room. The suite was separated into two smaller sleeping rooms with a bathroom in the middle. Kerri and Jessica would be sharing the other side, and since Mandy had decided to remain in Oregon with Matt for at least this first semester, Amber wasn't certain who would be sharing her space. It might be Lauren, but she hadn't heard for certain.

She knew they needed to go back to the car to get the rest of her things and help Kerri, and she turned to do so, but Seth gently took her hand and pulled her toward him. Taking her into his arms and offering her a comforting embrace, he said something that made the tears finally come. They had been sitting in her throat for the past five minutes, ever since she had snapped at him about dropping her quilt on the ground when he tried to carry everything at once. It was a very special quilt her grandmother had made for her many years ago and the most treasured possession she had from home. Seeing it lying on the dirty concrete in a patch of oil had been the last straw for her with all the things that had gone wrong today. She had been waiting for this day for close to a year, and it hadn't turned out the way she had always imagined.

"I'm sorry about the quilt," Seth said. "I'll find someplace to have it cleaned for you."

She didn't respond and let him hold her. This was so unlike her. She didn't get upset over little stuff like that. She rarely got upset at Seth period, and today of all days she wished she hadn't.

"It's okay," she said. "Don't worry about it. I can wash it here."

"I'm sorry it's been a long day," he apologized further. "We probably shouldn't have gone to the beach. I wasn't thinking about how tired we would be by now."

She allowed herself to relax in his arms. Maybe today hadn't gone like she would have planned it, but they were together. They were here, and she knew tomorrow would be a better day.

"We should help Kerri," she said, hearing her future sister-in-law leaving the room without invading their private moment. She felt more embarrassed about her outburst in front of Kerri than she did with Seth.

"One kiss first," he said.

She looked up at him and smiled. "You're not supposed to kiss me in here."

"Just for today."

She allowed the kiss, and Seth's sweet affection invaded her weary soul. His words brought comfort and helped her to feel safe and secure as they began this new phase of their life together.

"I promised I would take care of you, sweetheart. I promised your family. I promised you. And I promised myself. I'm sorry I didn't do very well with that today, but since it's my first day, I hope you can forgive me and trust me to do better tomorrow."

"You got us here, Seth. You got me here safely, and I shouldn't have gotten upset over something so minor. I'm sorry."

He kissed her on the forehead and stepped back, taking her hands into his and giving them a gentle squeeze. "We'll get the rest of your stuff and then you can have time to get settled. Are you hungry? I could go get you something."

"Just thirsty," she said. "I can get something from the vending machine."

"Are you feeling all right? You look like you have a headache."

"I do. I'll take something when we get back."

He appeared defeated once again, and she stepped into his arms. She hadn't wanted to tell him because he knew she only got headaches when she was having her period or when she was having a really stressful and frustrating day, and he already knew it wasn't that time of the month for her.

He felt reluctant to hold her in return, and she felt terrible for making him feel like a failure, because he wasn't. This wasn't his fault, it was hers. She had gotten her expectations too high about how fun this was going to be, forgetting about the long drive, her fragile emotions with leaving home for the first time, and never considering anything would go wrong with the car or there being road construction on the highway.

And then driving up the road leading to the college campus, she had allowed thoughts to enter her mind like, *What if this is a mistake? Maybe we're not supposed to be here, or maybe Seth is, but I'm not. What if I can't handle being on my own like this? I'm going to be here for months without seeing my family. What if Seth and I break up? Then what will I do?*

But she knew better. God had led them here. He had made His will very clear to them. He never said it would be easy, but He had confirmed they were on the right path—about school, about their future together, and about their personal journeys of seeking Him and letting Him take care of their needs. He would not fail them. He was here. And she could turn to Him with her weariness and disappointment and fears and frazzled emotions.

"I love you, Seth," she said, letting the tears fall once again. "I love you so much. Thank you for having the faith to get us here. Thank you for walking this path with me."

He held her tightly, and his words came out soft and emotional. "I love you too, Amber. I love you more than anything. Thank you for loving me back."

"It's easy to do, sweet thing," she whispered. "So easy."

"Except when I drop your quilt on the ground?" he teased her.

She stepped back and smiled. "I guess we're even now."

"Even?"

"I spilled Pepsi on you, you dropped my blanket." She laughed. "I'd say that makes us even."

"Does that mean it's my turn to break my wrist and cut my leg open?"

"I hope not," she said, giving him a sweet kiss and turning to drag him out of the room. "Your sister is going to be back before we get out of here."

They met her downstairs as they were about to step out of the elevator. Kerri had managed to find an empty cart and load the rest of their things onto it. The three of them rode up to the third floor and walked to the room at the end of the hall. Seth helped them unload everything and said he would take the cart back and let them have the rest of the evening to unpack.

"Good thinking on having us come today instead of tomorrow," Kerri said, giving him a hug. "And thanks for driving so much since I wasn't feeling up to it."

They had decided to come a day earlier than they originally planned because that would give them all of tomorrow to relax and explore the campus before orientation began on Monday, and that had been Seth's idea. Amber hadn't liked it too much at the time because it meant one less day with her family after being away from them all summer, but she knew now he was right.

Seth went to leave the room, but Amber suddenly didn't want him to go, at least not without her. She followed him into the hallway.

"Could we go for a walk?"

"We have tomorrow," he said. "You should rest, Amber."

"Please? I'll take some medicine for my headache and then we can go. Just for a little while? I've been with you all day, but not *with* you, you know?"

He smiled. "All right. But I'm saying good night at nine, and no arguing."

***

"I suppose Seth and Amber are at the campus by now," Matt said, checking the time.

"Probably," Amanda said, taking her browned marshmallow from the glowing fire and checking to see if it was equally done on all sides. "You want this one? It's perfect."

"You don't?" he asked.

"No. I'm full. I just like cooking them."

He smiled at her and took the warm marshmallow from the stick. "It is perfect. How do you do that? I always burn mine."

"Patience and timing," she said. "You have to be very patient."

He popped the gooey sugar-substance into his mouth before it began sticking to his fingers. He felt amazed it was already eight-thirty. This day with Amanda and her family, and yesterday when they spent time with Amber and Seth, had flown by compared to the previous days he'd been at home. After spending a few days together at camp during the final week, he had taken Amanda home on Friday and then spent six days with his family—and six lonely days without her. It wasn't that he hated being home, he just wanted her to be there too.

But he knew it wasn't fair to ask her to spend time with his family instead of hers after not seeing them for most of the summer, especially since his mom and dad didn't treat her the way she deserved. She was so special, sweet, and perfect for him. Why couldn't they see that? Why couldn't they believe he had honestly changed his ways and could have a respectable relationship with a respectable girl now?

"Are you certain you wouldn't rather be with them?" he asked, feeling a little bummed they weren't going to be at Lifegate with Amber and Seth this fall like they had originally planned.

"I'd like to be there, Matthew," she said, leaning against him in front of the glowing campfire. "But only if you're there too. If you're here, this is where I want to be."

"I'm sorry, Amanda."

"Don't be. God has us here for a reason. I truly believe that."

"Have you thought any more about where you want to go to school here?" They had discussed possibilities last week but hadn't talked about it since.

"I think going to community college is a good option. I've heard a lot of good things about Mount Hood. It's close, and they have all the classes I'd like to take."

"What would you think about us both going there?"

"It's a little far for you to have to come out every day. Why not go to one in Portland? Isn't there a community college really close to your house?"

"Yes, but you won't be there. I'd have to go all week without seeing you. I can ride MAX back and forth every day. It's not that far."

She looked up at him and smiled. "I'd love to have you there too. Maybe we could get into some of the same classes."

"Or at least have a similar schedule so we could have lunch together and be done at the same time."

"I brought the catalog along. We could look at it together tomorrow if you want."

"Yes. We'll do that."

"Are you planning to work too?"

He smiled and felt anxious to share his news with her. He had been waiting for the right moment. "Pastor John came by the house to talk to me this week."

"About what?"

16

"Filling one of the youth intern positions at the church. It doesn't pay much, but I'd really love to do that. I didn't apply for it like most people have to, he just offered it to me."

She smiled. "That's great, Matthew! Why didn't you tell me?"

He welcomed the hug she gave him and laughed at her question. "Just waiting for the right moment."

"What will you be doing?"

"Helping with planning, meeting with Pastor John and the other interns for training and discipleship, and then being at whatever youth events I'm assigned to—mostly Sunday night youth group and scheduled activities."

She had her own news to share. "I might be teaching piano lessons."

"Oh yeah?"

"I had a couple of families at church who asked me to teach their kids last spring, but I didn't have the time and knew I was going to be leaving in June anyway. But now that they know I'm going to be here this fall, they asked me again, and I told them I might be able to. I wanted to see what we decided about school and everything first."

"I think you should do it," he said.

Seeing the happy and peaceful expression on her face he had become used to over the summer, he remembered the unending joy he always felt with her before the difficulties of the past three weeks. Amanda brought a calmness and happy feeling to his heart whenever they were together, no matter what they were doing or what was going on around them.

Kissing her gently, he allowed himself to feel that joy again. Since his brother's death, her kisses had brought healing and comfort, and he had needed her closeness to help him through those difficult days. He would likely need her for that in the weeks and months to come, but right now he needed the joy. The joy of being in love with this amazing girl and knowing she felt the same way about him.

"I love loving you, Amanda."

"You do?" she said sweetly.

He smiled and kissed her again. "Yes, I do. Very much."

Chapter Two

Chad Williams had never felt so nervous in his life. He wasn't sure if he had made the right decision about asking Jessica to travel with him to the Lifegate campus today. Originally the plan had been for the two of them to go down with Seth, Amber, and Kerri today, which was Sunday, but their friends had decided to drive down together on Saturday instead. When he called Jessica to tell her, she said she couldn't go until Sunday because her mom and dad had planned a going-away party for her, and she didn't want to bail on them or make them change their plans.

Jessica had told the four of them to go ahead, that she would fly down on Sunday and he could come pick her up at the airport, but Chad had offered to wait the extra day. He felt okay about the decision at the time, supposing it would be a good chance for them to have more time together. He and Jessica had been officially dating for three weeks now, but they had only gone out once when it was just the two of them.

That had been three weeks ago—two weeks before their summer at Camp Laughing Water ended. Chad had confessed his feelings for her, and she had expressed her mutual interest in exploring a relationship beyond friendship with him. He had taken her to the reservoir for the afternoon where they had taken a long walk beside the water, found a quiet spot to sit and talk for two hours, and then he had taken her to dinner that evening.

It had been a pleasant day, and he knew they had gotten to know each other better. He'd had every intention of taking her out again the following weekend, but because of Matt's brother being tragically lost, they had spent the day with the rest of their friends instead. They had gone for a short walk on the beach together and also had a few times alone last weekend on the staff retreat, but they had both kept it more friendship-oriented than romantic, and he had enjoyed their time for what it was.

He hadn't kissed her yet. He liked her a lot and felt comfortable around her, but he didn't see himself falling in love overnight. His heart had become too cautious for that, and after hearing about her previous relationships, he didn't think she would mind taking a slow pace.

He hadn't been worried about today until he talked to Seth last night and heard about the difficult time they'd had because of the highway being under construction. It had taken them an extra hour to get there, and Chad knew there would be a lot of weekend traffic today too. He had never driven so far on his own, and he had a fear of getting them lost or having his car break down in no-man's-land.

Walking from his car to the front door of her house, he had another reason to feel nervous. He would be meeting her family for the first time. She had told him it would be fine, but he expected them to be cautious about letting her set off for California with a guy they had never met before. He wanted to make a good first impression, but he wasn't sure how. All he could do was be himself, but would they like him for who he was?

Taking a deep breath, he rang the doorbell and breathed a silent prayer. God always upheld him when he looked to Him for that, but today he couldn't shake the anxiety.

Her dad, Chad assumed, opened the door and greeted him politely. "Good morning. You must be Chad."

"I am," he said, reaching out to shake the hand offered to him.

"Good to meet you," Mr. Shaw said. "Come on in. I think she's about ready. We kept her up late last night, so she's getting a bit of a late start."

From what he had gathered from Jessica, he knew she had a close family. They had gone through some difficult times when her older brother had a few rebellious years and then she began to follow in his footsteps, but after she had turned her life over to Jesus prior to her senior year of high school, she'd had a better relationship with her mom and dad and had been praying for her brother and seen him take steps to do the same. They both had chosen to stay at home and go to Portland State rather than going off to college somewhere else and living away from home, so Jessie leaving to attend a far-off college for her second year was a big deal for them, especially since they had been doing so well as a family.

"Hello, you must be Chad," a woman who looked like an older version of Jessica said, coming down the wide, spiral staircase to greet him.

"Yes," he said, stepping forward to shake her hand also, but getting a hug instead.

"She's almost ready," Mrs. Shaw laughed. "I think giving her one less day to pack would have been a good thing after all."

Chad laughed, but her words reminded him of another concern. He had put all of his stuff in the back seat of the car and left the trunk space for Jessie, but it wasn't much. He hoped she wouldn't have to leave anything behind.

"You can go on up," Mrs. Shaw added. "She has most of it ready so we can get started on getting it into the car. And I told her we could ship that one box to her, so if you know it won't fit, don't bother trying. I'm sure she'll survive for a few days without it."

Chad headed up the stairs and felt relieved about the way Mr. and Mrs. Shaw had welcomed his arrival, but he felt nervous about seeing Jessie too. He hadn't seen her since Monday. He had talked to her on the phone several times, but seeing her face-to-face always brought a different feeling to his heart. Sort of a nervous, self-conscious, happy feeling. Her beauty mesmerized him, and her sweetness made him want to say, 'Your wish is my command.'

Her room was easy to locate with two suitcases sitting in the hallway, and he knocked on the open door. Neither of her parents had followed him up. He could see her bed had stuff on it, including a folded comforter, blankets, and a pillow, but he saw no sign of Jessica.

He stepped into the room and could hear a hairdryer running. He looked toward the sound, seeing the partially closed door of what he assumed was a bathroom attached to her large bedroom. A few times during the summers when they had both been on staff at the camp, he had been with Seth and Kerri when they dropped off Jessica or picked her up, so he had seen the neighborhood she lived in and the upscale home, but stepping inside and being surrounded by the fine things she was used to drove home the reality a bit more that her family had money—lots of it, and his didn't.

They weren't poor, and he had no complaints—no needs that he had to go without, but he knew he and Jessie had differences in the way they had been raised, and the money-thing was something that worried him. He wouldn't know what to get her for her birthday, let alone be prepared anytime soon to take care of her. Seth was getting married next summer because his parents had the financial means to help him do that, but he was on his own from here on out. Grants and a scholarship were paying for his education, but he was going to need a job to help him with personal expenses and having any kind of money to spend on his girlfriend.

He wasn't sure if he should let her know he was here or just begin taking her things downstairs. He waited a moment and then heard someone's voice coming from the hallway.

"Hey, you must be Chad."

He turned and saw a guy he knew must be her brother. Jessie had talked about Daniel a lot during the time they had spent together, and he knew they were close. Daniel was going to be a senior at Portland State this year. He had struggled during his first two years of college, academically and behavior-wise, but he was doing well now and would be graduating in the spring.

"You must be Daniel," Chad said, stepping over to shake his hand.

"That's me. Would you like a hand here?"

"Sure," he said. "I guess all of this goes."

Daniel picked up two of the suitcases, and Chad was about to grab the large box he thought might fit, but Jessica's voice stopped him.

"Hey, Chad. I didn't know you were here."

He turned and saw she appeared to be ready. She was wearing capri pants and a light blue shirt. Her hair looked freshly washed, and the fragrance of something sweet-smelling was either coming from the bathroom or from Jessie herself.

"I just got here," he said. "We were going to take this stuff out. Is that all right?"

"We?"

He glanced back and saw Daniel had disappeared with the suitcases. "Me and your brother."

"That's fine," she said, stepping closer and saying what her mom had said about the box. "If that doesn't fit, they can ship it to me."

"I think it might," he said. "We can try."

She smiled at him. "Can I have a hug first, or are we in too big of a hurry?"

He smiled and turned to face her fully. "I'm in no hurry."

She stepped into his arms. He held her gently and was surprised by her words.

"I've missed you."

"Have you?"

"Yes. Don't sound so surprised."

"I've missed you too."

"Have you?" she challenged him.

"Yes," he said. He was used to seeing her every day and had been missing her since she had driven away last week. "I'm glad I decided to wait for you."

"Me too," she said, stepping out of his arms but not putting a great amount of distance between them. "I think I would be nervous about having to get on a plane and fly away from home for the first time. This is better."

He hoped she was right, but he kept his insecurities to himself. "And you get to take more stuff," he teased her.

"Yes," she laughed. "That too."

He turned and reached for the box once again. It wasn't terribly heavy, and he knew it was most likely filled with clothing. "You know, I heard a rumor they have washers and dryers there in the dorms."

She gave him a look. "I have been very good about living out of a suitcase all summer," she defended herself. "But I'm a little tired of it, so deal with it, buddy."

Something about Jessie always brought out a playful side of him few had the ability to do. One of them was his younger half-sister, Keisha, and the other was Kerri Kirkwood. But he was definitely having feelings for Jessica that went beyond a sisterly type of friendship.

He stepped back and leaned down to whisper something in her ear. "My name isn't Buddy, it's Chad.

I don't expect much from my girlfriends, but remembering my name is one of them."

"I know your name, Chad Michael Williams," she countered. "And I want to know a lot more than that."

Chad considered himself to be a private person and knew he had been holding back with Jessie so far. She had shared a lot about herself and had seemed content to do a lot of the talking. He had remained quiet and kept things to himself he'd had the opportunity to say but hadn't. But he knew he needed to change that if he expected to have her as his girlfriend on an extended basis.

"You can ask me anything today," he said, sounding more comfortable with that than he felt.

"Anything?"

"Anything."

She smiled at him for now, but Chad had the feeling she was going to hold him to that promise.

***

Kerri finished putting away her clothes and slid the second empty suitcase under her bed. She could hear Amber talking to Seth on the phone on her side of the dorm-suite and knew they were discussing what they were going to do this afternoon. Whatever they decided on, Kerri supposed they would ask her to come along, and she was debating about spending the day with them or doing her own thing.

She knew Lauren would be coming sometime this afternoon, and she wanted to be here when she arrived. Chad and Jess wouldn't be here until later, and she said a little prayer for them they wouldn't have any problems on the drive down like she, Amber, and Seth had encountered yesterday. In a way she could see how a difficult day would create a bonding experience between them like it seemed to have done for her brother and Amber, but at this early stage in their relationship, she knew a relatively easy and smooth day would be better.

She knew them both well enough to know they could decide this relationship wasn't meant to be, but for different reasons. Chad didn't feel worthy of a girl like Jessica—not smart enough, not rich enough, not social enough; and Jessie was just plain scared. She had given herself to three different guys in high school who had left her with serious emotional scars. One her sophomore year and two her junior year. She had dated very little since turning her life around, which had been a good thing in the beginning. She needed time to heal, find her worth in God, and keep herself out of the arms of selfish, manipulative guys.

But this summer Jessie had confessed she had been using the 'I'm not ready' excuse a little too much, turning down perfectly great guys out of fear of getting hurt more than being cautious. Kerri supposed that was for the best because it had left her available when Chad finally got around to telling her how he felt, but Kerri would hate to see her push Chad away for that reason. If Jessie didn't want it for other reasons that were legitimate, she would support her in that, but she wasn't going to let Jessie run away from someone like Chad just because she was scared.

Chad was too special for that. He had always been a nice guy. She had known him since middle school when he and Seth had played soccer together. Seth and Chad had become good friends that year, and just about any friend of her twin brother she had gotten to know well too. One of the things she had always liked about Chad was his easy-going and quiet personality. But he had been burned for it during their junior year when he dated Rhonda.

Kerri had *U.S. History* with Rhonda and Chad, and she had watched Rhonda flirt her way into Chad's affection, seduce him into a fast-moving, intimate relationship, cheat on him twice in four months time, and then turn her back and completely ignore him without any sign of remorse. Both she and Seth had tried to warn him, but it had only caused him to withdraw from their friendship, so Kerri had backed off.

And then one weekend his life had completely changed. About a week after Rhonda had broken his heart for the second time, he ran into Seth after school, and Seth had invited him to come on the retreat their youth group was having. Chad said yes, and that weekend he had found Jesus. Or maybe Jesus had found him. Found him in his brokenness, picked him up, and carried him straight into His Love.

Kerri loved to hear Chad talk about it. He had one of the most sincere and simple testimonies of finding God she'd ever heard, and it wasn't just something he talked about, it was something he lived. He embraced the love and grace of God in a way that compelled her to do the same. She had thought she knew God before that, and she had. She knew about Him. She knew much more than Chad in an intellectual sense. But Chad had flown past all the Sunday school lessons and clichés about God and shot straight to God's heart. A heart that loved him just because, and Chad had clung to the truth in a way that completely transformed him overnight and made her take a deeper look at God's love for herself.

He was still quiet, even shy at times. But if Jessie could get him talking about God, Kerri knew she would never shut him up.

Chapter Three

Carrying her laundry basket filled with miscellaneous items, Colleen entered the hallway of her second-story dorm room and stepped into the third room on the right. Setting the basket on the bare mattress beside all of her bedding, she went to close the door and then decided to open the window before she started unpacking.

Her roommate hadn't arrived yet, and she wondered what she would be like and hoped they got along well. Megan West from camp had said she would be coming today, and she planned to drop by her room later and say hi, but for now she was content to be alone and get settled. Deciding to start with setting up her desk, she opened her supplies box and began placing the various items on the desk beside the window.

She felt tempted to call Blake while she had privacy, but she didn't know if she could handle only having a few minutes with him while he was on his way to California. His sister would be with him, and if she ended up crying over the phone, she wouldn't want him to be dealing with that while he was driving and not be able to talk more freely.

He told her he would call tonight but to call him sooner if she needed that. She had already talked to him this morning, so she supposed she could wait a few more hours, but she missed him. They'd had a really great time at Shasta Lake with his family last week, and telling him good-bye for an unknown amount of time on Thursday afternoon had been difficult—even more so than she had expected.

She didn't know how she had fallen in love with him so fast. Three months ago she'd never met him; two months ago she didn't think of him as anything besides some guy at camp; and one month ago she had been trying to convince herself she wasn't ready for another relationship after he expressed an interest in dating her.

But now here she was, just three weeks after letting him kiss her for the first time, and she couldn't go a day without crying because of the void his absence had left. She had no other reason to be crying. Her life was great. She was starting college, something she had been looking forward to for a long time. She knew she was at the school where God wanted her right now. She didn't feel certain of her future plans, but she was at peace with the unknown and waiting for God to lead her. She was away from her family, but she felt good about her prospects of making good friends here.

The only thing missing was Blake. He planned to come visit her, but they had decided to wait to set a definite date until they knew when would be the best time for both of them. Still feeling tempted to call him, she decided to call Amber instead.

Her phone rang before she picked it up, and she supposed it was her mom checking to see if she had gotten here all right. Her mom and dad had offered to help with finding her room and getting settled, but she had wanted to come on her own and do this by herself.

The caller wasn't her mom, however, and she smiled.

"Hey, are you there yet?" Blake's voice greeted her.

"I'm here," she said. "You're not supposed to be calling me now."

He laughed. "We're about to head into the mountains, and I thought I'd try you before we got there. This is the last spot for a good connection for awhile."

She didn't say anything. She wanted to, but she didn't know what to say. He had called her yesterday too, but she found it difficult to talk to him on the phone.

"I miss you, sweetheart," he said sincerely, and she knew he was likely stopped along the highway somewhere where he could talk to her privately. "I just wanted to hear your voice. Are you okay?"

"Yes."

"Do you miss me?"

"Yes."

"Really?"

She laughed. "Yes! You're about to make me cry."

"Don't cry," he said. "Just know that I love you and I'm thinking about you."

"I'm thinking about you too. I almost called you when I got here."

"Why didn't you?"

She didn't answer. Her excuses were lame, and she knew it.

"Don't do that, Colleen. Don't be sensible when it comes to us. When you feel like calling me, do it. And if I don't answer, then leave a message, and I'll call you back, always. Don't think for a second you can quietly fade out of my life, or what we started this summer isn't meant to last. I *love* you. Do you believe that?"

"Yes."

He didn't respond, and she knew why. He never settled for quick answers. Searching her heart for a moment, she admitted her fears.

"And exactly how long are you planning to do that?"

"Do what?" he teased.

She smiled. "Love me."

"For a very, very long time."

"Promise?"

"I promise."

"I need you to keep telling me that, okay?"

"If you keep believing it, I will."

"Are you still going to call me later?"

"Absolutely."

"It's going to take time for me to get used to talking to you on the phone. I like it better when I can see you. We might have to set up some video chat times."

"You can imagine I'm better-looking this way."

"Is that what you're doing?" She laughed. "Imagining I'm more beautiful?"

"Not possible. I can't imagine anyone more beautiful than you, and besides, I'm looking at your picture right now, so it's almost like you're here, but the kissing isn't quite the same."

She smiled. She missed his kisses too. "You're a great kisser."

"I am?"

"Yes, definitely. You take my breath away, Blake Coleman."

"You'll be getting more real soon. I promise."

"I can't wait," she said, hearing someone open the door behind her. She turned and saw a girl stepping into the room. She smiled and went to help her open the door fully.

"Is someone there?" Blake asked.

"Yes, my new roommate, I think."

"Okay, I'll let you go."

"Hang on a second," she said, taking one of the bags from the girl and carrying it into the room. "I'm not through with you yet."

She quickly introduced herself to her roommate and asked if she had more to bring up. "Yes," the blond girl said, speaking with a European accent. "I'm Sonya."

"Nice to meet you," she said. "I'll just be a minute, and then I'll help you with the rest."

"All right. Thank you. I need to use the restroom, and then I'll come back."

Once Sonya had stepped out, Colleen spoke to Blake once again. "You still there?"

"I'm here."

"What were we talking about?"

"Kissing."

"Oh yeah. My favorite topic."

"Three weeks, baby. I'm coming in three weeks."

"When did you decide that?"

"Just now."

"I can't wait."

"I love you, Colleen. So much. Don't forget, okay?"

"I won't. I love you too."

***

Lauren had to smile as she watched her brother talking on the phone with Colleen. She couldn't hear what he was saying because he was standing outside the car, but she could see the smile on his face and a look she had never seen from him before. She had been amazed when she saw Colleen and Blake together this week. They didn't just like each other. They were falling in love. And one thought kept running through her mind whenever she saw her brother with that look in his eyes. *Don't let Colleen break his heart, Jesus. Please, don't let that happen.*

Her thoughts turned to Adam. She hadn't seen him for a week now, and a huge part of her still wondered how she had ended up with him. She had liked him all summer, but being his girlfriend had never been anything more than a fantasy until three weeks ago. Now it was real. It was happening, but she had no idea why.

Blake opened the door and got into the car with a peaceful smile on his face. She laughed at him. A joyful laugh she couldn't contain. She had never seen him like this.

"She misses me," he said.

"Like there was any doubt. Of course she misses you."

"She didn't miss Chris."

Lauren kissed him on the cheek. "She wasn't in love with him."

"Then why on earth is she in love with me?" he laughed. "Me? That's crazy!"

"Not that crazy," she said, reaching for her seat belt and pulling it across her body. "Give me one good reason why she wouldn't fall for you."

He didn't answer that, and Blake pulled out of the parking space at the rest area to head back to the freeway. Lauren heard her own words echoing in her mind—*Give yourself one good reason Adam wouldn't fall in love with you.* She had about a million.

Plain. Ordinary. Nothing special. Not beautiful. Quiet. Unexciting. Average student. No big dreams and goals. Not talented...

"Do you want to call Adam before we head into these mountains?" Blake interrupted her thoughts. "If he's not too far behind us, we could meet him for dinner."

Lauren glanced at her purse. No, she didn't want to call him. She did. She didn't. Blake made the decision for her, reaching inside the top pouch and handing it to her. Taking the phone, she went ahead. She didn't want Blake to think there was any reason she didn't want to, because she did. She just felt nervous and was glad when she got his voice mail instead of a live response.

"Hey, this is Adam. Sorry I missed your call. Leave me a message, and I'll get back to you."

She didn't leave a message.

"No answer?" Blake asked.

"No."

"You should have left him a message," he said.

"I didn't know what to say."

"How about, 'I miss you.'?"

"I'd rather talk to him."

"Do you miss him?"

"Yes."

"Why?"

She laughed. "Because I do."

"Because you love him?"

"I'm not sure about that," she replied honestly. "I like him very much."

"How was your time with him at Silver Falls? I never got a chance to ask you."

"Good," she said.

"Just good?"

She smiled. That had been a very good day. A perfect day. "It was very good," she said simply.

Her phone rang and she answered it.

"You called me," Adam said.

"I did."

"Where are you?"

"Near Mt. Shasta. Where are you?"

"Klamath Falls."

"Klamath Falls?"

He laughed. "It's a good thing you didn't wait for me. My truck had a flat tire this morning, so I had to have it fixed before I got out of Bend."

"Do you want us to wait for you?"

"No. You go ahead. Get settled and then we can have time together this evening. I have something to tell you, but I'll wait until then."

"I miss you," she said.

"I miss you too, Angel. Have a kiss waiting for me when I get there, all right?"

"All right. Drive safe."

"I will. See you in about six hours."

"Okay, bye."

Lauren clicked off the phone and had a familiar happy feeling in her heart. She was amazed by the way Adam made her feel. She hoped she wasn't making too much of it, but unless Adam was lying to her about the way he felt too, she couldn't see any reason why he couldn't be the guy she could marry someday. Except for the fact he was her first boyfriend, they were only eighteen, they'd been dating for three weeks, he was great and she was...

"You all right?" Blake asked.

She put the phone back in her purse and smiled. "Yes." She explained about him being farther behind than they thought he might be, and then she reached for something else in her purse: the letter he had written to her a couple of weeks ago and given to her after their second date. Taking it out of the envelope, she read her favorite parts and allowed his words to remind her why she had reason to hope this wasn't going to be ending between them anytime soon.

You're the girl I've spent the last two years praying for, Angel. The girl I asked God to have wait for me and I promised to wait for. I've tried to put other girls in that place, but this time I know it's not me that's doing it, it's God. When He opened my eyes to see you, it was like a lightning bolt and a gentle whisper; like a crashing ocean wave and the rising sun; like nothing I'd ever imagined and something so familiar I barely gave it a second thought...

I've been feeling a little lost about going to college. I'm not sure what I want to study. I don't feel God leading me in any particular direction, but suddenly that seems so secondary. Whatever paths God takes us on from here, I just hope they're side-by-side and eventually will merge into one.

Taking out her notebook from her backpack, she had some thoughts, and she wrote them out:

I was seeking Him
And I found you.
I asked Him for blessings
And He sent you.
I wished for love
And He gave me you.

I was seeking Him;
His love and His truth
And I have seen it
Through you and in us;
Like a beacon of light
It all seems so clear.

He says I'll walk the streets of gold
A path of beauty, purity and love;
I've found that with you
It's heaven on earth
God's love gift to me
Is you, my love. It's you.

So I won't let go
When those voices say
'He's not for you'
because I believe you are;
For I was seeking Him
And I found you

Chapter Four

"Are you getting hungry?" Chad asked, glancing over at Jessica who had slowly stirred from sleep. It was past lunchtime, and they were approaching a small town along I-5. So far their trip had been uneventful. Jessie was tired and had been sleeping for an hour.

"Yeah," she said. "Sorry I slept so long. You could have woken me up."

"I was all right. Where would you like to eat?"

"Anywhere is fine," she said.

"McDonald's or Taco Bell?"

"Yes. Either."

"What's your favorite?"

She smiled. "I said I didn't care."

"But what's your favorite?"

"Do they have Dairy Queen?"

"Yes."

"That's my favorite."

He didn't say anything else and pulled off the highway and followed the signs to the local Dairy Queen.

"What's your favorite?" she asked once they had gotten out of the car and were walking to the door.

"I like Dairy Queen."

"But what's your favorite?"

"I like anything."

"Chad! I told you my favorite. You have to tell me yours."

"I don't have a favorite."

She gave up. He laughed when she told him what to order for her in an aggravated way and then left him to go use the bathroom. After he placed their order, he found a table to sit at and waited for their number to be called. Glancing around at the other diners, he knew this was mostly an all-white community. A young girl was staring at him from the adjacent booth as if she had never seen a person with dark skin in real-life. He smiled at her, and she looked away, but she kept glancing back.

Growing up in Portland and living in an ethnically diverse area of the city, he hadn't experienced much of that. He hadn't felt the sting of prejudice like he knew many African-Americans and other minorities faced. He didn't see himself as different, because where he'd grown up, everyone was different. He had gone to school with white kids, black kids, Asian kids, Hispanics, and many other races and mixes of races, and most of them had grown up to see no color. They were just his friends, and he was theirs.

He had been teased and called names now and then, but not any more so than kids who were picked on because they were fat or nerds or wore glasses or didn't wear the right clothes. But outside of his familiar and safe neighborhood, the lines were more clearly drawn, and although he hadn't experienced much of it, he could see in a small Oregon town like this, he probably would.

He wondered what he would encounter at Lifegate. Since three of his closest friends who were going there were rich white kids, he was expecting more of the same, but he tried not to worry about it. Seth, Kerri, and Jessica had never treated him differently, and most of the people he had gotten to know at church and camp had treated him well and with more love than he had ever known from anyone besides his own family. He had every reason to believe he would encounter the same at the small Christian college, even if he was the only one with a better than average California tan.

When Jessie returned from the bathroom and sat across from him in the booth, he could see the other diners trying not to look their way, but they did. He tried to ignore everything around him but Jessie, figuring he would only have to deal with what other people thought if they said something to him directly. He didn't know if Jessica sensed it until after they had gotten their food and began eating.

"Don't let it bother you, Chad. It doesn't bother me."

He smiled, wondering how she could read his mind when he was doing his best to not think about it.

"They're just looking at you because you're so beautiful," he said, tossing her a wink.

Neither of them said anything else about it, but Chad couldn't help but breathe an inward sigh when they got back into the car. He had been praying the entire time they were inside no one would say or do anything to them, not so much for his sake, but

Jessie's. He would never want to be the reason for someone saying or doing something hateful to her, and he began to wonder if he could do this.

Maybe them dating was a mistake. Maybe he was inviting trouble. Maybe it would be better to tell her he only wanted to be friends. Surely there were plenty of guys at Lifegate for her to choose from. Good guys. Christian guys who would be getting in line to win her affection. Who was he to be dating this beautiful girl who made his knees go weak? What did he possibly have to offer her?

"Are you okay?" she asked once they were back on the freeway.

He had put in a CD and turned it up to block out the silence between them. He felt like he should be more talkative, but he didn't know what to say. He wanted to tell her what he was thinking. He wanted to share his fears, but he didn't know how.

"I'm fine," he lied. "Are you?"

"Yeah, fine," she said, but she didn't look away.

He took a deep breath and let it out slowly.

Be honest with her, Chad. It's all right.

"That was weird for me," he said. "I'm not used to it, and I'm still shaking."

"You mean in the restaurant?"

"Yes."

"Nothing happened. No one said anything."

"I know, but they could have. I know I shouldn't let it bother me, and it doesn't, but it scares me."

"What scares you?" she said, reaching over to take his hand.

"Someone hurting you."

"Jesus protects me, Chad. He'll protect us."

46

He knew she was right. He had read and studied the Bible enough to know God *promises* to protect those who trust in Him. And he knew that referred to this as much as anything else.

"I'm a young, pretty girl, Chad," she went on. "I don't need to have a boyfriend who's a different race than me to give some sick guy out there a reason to stalk me, or attack me, or something even worse. But I can't live in fear. I can't be afraid of those things, or of leaving home, or of anything that keeps me from living my life the way I believe God leads me to live it."

He was reminded of God's hand in bringing them together. Last summer when he had first begun to feel attracted to her, he didn't think he could open himself up to another relationship. But he felt God telling him to not shut out the possibility.

Not yet, Chad. This isn't the right time, he'd clearly heard Jesus telling him. *But maybe someday. Maybe next summer. Wait on Me, and I will show you.*

"Do you believe it's right for us to be together?" he asked. "I don't mean about the black and white thing, but do you think this is what God wants for you? To be with me?"

"Yes. Me and Jesus have had some good talks about you."

"Have you?"

"Yes. I don't date much. You know that."

"And that's why? Because God has been telling you not to?"

"Mostly, yes. There was one guy earlier this year I pushed away because I was scared, but then when God brought you into my life, I couldn't do that."

"Why?"

"Because you're everything I'm looking for. Everything God has told me to wait for."

He waited to see if she would elaborate on that. When she didn't, he knew this was one of those moments he had something to say along the same lines, but— *No buts, Chad. Just tell her.*

"I feel that way too," he said. "About you, I mean."

"You think this is what God wants?"

"Yes. He showed me that this summer."

"How did He show you?"

"I've liked you since last year, but God told me to wait and see if He brought us back together, and I was fine with that because I was scared of it anyway."

"What were you afraid of?"

He knew, but he had a difficult time saying it.

"Because of what people might think?" she asked.

"No. That was an excuse, but it wasn't what I was afraid of."

She remained silent, waiting for him to say it. He didn't know why the pain seemed so fresh. It had been a year and a half since Rhonda had hurt him so deeply and made a complete fool out of him. And he hadn't even been in love with her. Not really. He thought she cared about him, but when he discovered she was just using him, he felt alone and worthless. It had turned into a good thing because at his lowest point, God had been able to reach his heart, but still, it wasn't something he wanted to experience again. He couldn't imagine Jessie being the liar and manipulator Rhonda had been, but he'd never seen Rhonda that way until the reality of it smacked him in the face.

He had talked about it that first Saturday when Jessie asked him about his most recent relationship, but he had remained emotionless and Jessica already knew about it in a general way through Kerri. She hadn't known he hadn't dated since, but he had covered by saying, "I needed to get close to God and become really solid in that before I got involved in another relationship."

That was true, but not quite the whole truth.

***

Jessica thought seriously about the way she felt about Chad. She knew what he was afraid of because she was afraid of it too: Getting hurt again. She had done everything she could to avoid it, and she believed in the choices she had made to protect herself during the last two years. But at some point she was going to have to go beyond what she could control and trust God to take care of her heart.

And the truth was, she knew Chad was worth the risk. Maybe he wasn't the one she was meant to spend the rest of her life with, or maybe he was. He was a very special person. Someone she liked being with, someone she felt safe with, someone who had a close relationship with God. She actually felt more afraid of hurting him than of getting hurt herself. And she would never intentionally hurt him, but it could happen.

"I know, Chad," she finally said. "You don't have to say it."

They rode in silence, and for her it was a comfortable silence. One of the things she liked about

Chad was his quietness, but she could see him becoming more uncomfortable as the minutes passed. She wanted to change the subject and get his mind on something else, but she knew she needed to give him some kind of indication he had something to hope for with her.

She hadn't heard God telling her otherwise, so she decided it was time to take a chance on love if that's what Chad wanted too, and she was pretty sure he did. When they came to the next rest area along the highway, she asked him to stop. He did so and they both got out of the car to use the restroom. Jessica thought about what she wanted to say and asked God to help her say it in the right way. When she returned to the parking area, Chad was already in the car waiting for her, but she went to his side and spoke to him through the open window.

"Could we go for a walk?" she asked.

"Sure."

She waited for him to get out and then took his hand and led them down a path that wove its way through a grassy area where people could sit and rest or have a picnic. It felt good to walk around after sitting so much today, but that wasn't her main reason for asking him.

Seeing an empty picnic table underneath a grove of trees, she stepped onto the grass and led him there, sitting down on the bench and waiting for him to join her. She had been comfortable with the time they'd spent together thus far, and she appreciated Chad's non-pushy displays of affection. She wouldn't have been opposed to him kissing her before now, but she was glad he hadn't tried to go there yet.

But with them heading off to college together, her seeing a vulnerable side of Chad just now, and knowing he needed reassurance she wanted this and understood his fears, she suddenly felt the need to do more than hold his hand and say what she wanted to say. She wanted into his space. It was a scary thought because getting into his space would mean letting him into hers, but she knew it was time.

Seeing the comfortable distance he left between them on the wooden bench, she smiled at him and moved closer. They had sat facing away from the table with their backs to the main area by the restrooms, so even though they weren't alone here, it was enough for her to feel like they had some privacy. She gently leaned against him. He had a broad, well-defined chest and was quite tall, but his length was more in his legs, so sitting with him like this, she was able to lay her head on his shoulder with her eyes falling naturally on his exposed neck and beautiful brown skin above his shirt collar.

He didn't resist her, and his arm draped around her back and held her gently against him. His deliberate gentleness gave her a warm and safe feeling, and she knew she didn't just need this right now. She wanted it.

"I want this, Chad. I want to be in your life like this. And I want you to treat me like your girlfriend, because I am. I don't want anything from you except something genuine. Something real. Something that matters to both of us we can enjoy, and be ourselves, and feel safe with each other."

She expected him to say he was scared, but he didn't. He held her close to him and didn't say anything, but she took his silence as an acceptance of what she had said, not a rejection of it. Lifting her head from his shoulder, she looked into his soft brown eyes. "Is that what you want too? Is this comfortable for you? You and me like this?"

He smiled and took her hand from where she had rested it gently on his thigh. Lifting it to his lips, he kissed her fingers and held them against his chest. She could feel his heart beating through his lightweight cotton shirt, and she returned his relaxed smile. He kissed her cheek gently and then whispered in her ear.

"I want this, Jessie. You and me like this—if you want it too."

Closing her eyes, she felt his lips brush her cheek and then caress her lips very gently. She returned the tender affection and felt her heart opening after being closed to this kind of intimacy for a long time, and yet it was beyond anything she had ever experienced before.

It wasn't just a kiss, it was a caring kind of tenderness. And it wasn't just any guy, it was Chad. And it was amazing.

Chapter Five

Kerri was reading through her official Lifegate Student Handbook when she heard a knock on the door of her dorm room. Getting off her bed, she went to answer it and squealed when she saw who it was.

"Lauren! You made it."

"We did," she said, and Kerri saw Blake appear as well with several bags and suitcases in hand.

"Are you in this room?"

"Yes. I called on Friday to confirm it, and they said it hadn't been reassigned to anyone else, but they won't have my keys and everything ready until tomorrow."

"Come on in," she said, feeling excited Lauren would be rooming with them in Mandy's place. She'd had a lot of good friends over the years, but she had formed a unique connection with Lauren this summer, and she was looking forward to having that kind of time with her here too.

"Over here?" Lauren asked, pointing to the side of the room she would be sharing with Amber.

"Yes," Kerri confirmed, taking one of her bags from her and leading the way. "Do you have more?"

"Just my blankets," she said.

"I'll go get them," Blake said after setting down everything in his arms.

Lauren thanked her brother and turned back, giving her a hug now that she didn't have her hands full.

"I'm so glad you're here," Kerri said. "How was your drive?"

"Fine."

"Is Adam here too?"

"No, he got a late start this morning, so he probably won't be here for another couple of hours."

"Oh, that's too bad," she teased her. "I guess I get you all to myself until then."

"Where's Amber?"

"One guess."

Lauren laughed and didn't bother to answer that. "And Jessica?"

"Not here yet. I think they should be soon unless they get caught in that construction traffic."

"Her and Chad?"

"Yes."

"Why didn't they come with you guys?"

"Jessica's family had a going-away thing planned for her last night, and Chad decided to wait until today to come down too. I think that will be good for them to have some extended time together."

"I think you're right about that," she said. "Have you had dinner?"

"No, not yet."

"Neither have we. Do you want to go get something with us?"

"Sure. Do you want to get settled here first?"

"No, I can do it later. I'm hungry now!"

After Blake brought her bedding up, they took his stuff to his room and left for town to get dinner. Meals weren't being served in the cafeteria until tomorrow morning. They went to the pizza place where Blake had been working for the past two years and was planning to again this year. So was Seth, and Kerri wasn't surprised when her brother and Amber showed up. Apparently Seth and Blake had already talked about possibly eating here tonight, and Blake took Seth to meet his boss and pick up an application to work here too.

Kerri noticed other college students scattered around the sizable dining area. This was obviously a popular place, and she wondered if they were Lifegate students too. She asked Lauren what she thought, and Lauren informed her of something she didn't know.

"They're probably from Humboldt," she said.

"What's Humboldt?"

"Humboldt University. It's a state school here in town. Some of the college students at church that Blake is friends with go there."

"So this really is a college town then, huh?"

"Yes. Kevin goes there too."

"Who's Kevin?"

"One of the guys Blake works with here. He's actually the owner's son, and I've met him when we've come to visit Blake before."

Seth and Blake returned to the table then, and Seth had an application in hand and an extra one for Chad who would also be looking for a job.

"What have you been doing today?" Kerri asked Seth.

"We found a nice beach to walk on. It's not so windy today, so that took up a good hour, and then we explored the town a bit. How about you?"

"I got unpacked and waited for Lauren to get here. I read some of the student handbook. Did you know they don't allow displays of affection between couples on campus?"

Seth stopped his writing and looked up with a deer-in-the-headlights look. She tried to keep a straight face but cracked up laughing.

"You'd better be kidding," he said, appearing to realize she was.

"Gotcha!"

He shook his head and went back to his writing. "That would not be cool. I've had enough of that rule to last me for the rest of my life."

"What rule?" Amber asked. She had been in the restroom and had just returned to the table.

"Nothing, sweetheart," he said, leaning over to give her a kiss.

Kerri was glad to see they had made up from their little moment of frustration with each other last night. It had been a long day, and she didn't blame Amber for getting upset about her quilt, but it had surprised her. Amber was rarely mad at anybody, especially Seth. But it had been sort of comforting to know even Amber had moments like that. Kerri felt like she had at least one a week, but she was trying to have more patience with people. It was not one of her strengths.

Amber asked what she had done today, and she was in the middle of telling her what she'd already told Seth when someone came over to the table and caught Blake's attention. He appeared to work here.

He had a Tony's Pizza t-shirt on and a white apron tied around his waist over his jeans. Blake stood up as soon as he saw him.

"Kevin, my man!" Blake said rather exuberantly, giving Kevin an immediate heartfelt hug. "How are you? Good to see you."

Kevin didn't respond with words. He smiled and seemed glad to see Blake.

"You remember Lauren, my sister?" he asked.

Kevin nodded, and Lauren said 'hi' to him, rising from her chair to give him a hug, which Kevin returned somewhat shyly without saying anything. For a moment Kerri wondered if Kevin was deaf because he hadn't spoken yet, but then when Lauren asked him something, he responded in a normal voice.

"Do I get a rematch on pinball?" she asked.

"Yes," he said, reaching into his pocket and pulling out some quarters. "My treat."

"And this is Amber and Seth and Kerri," Blake went on. "Some of my new friends at school this year."

Seth stood up and reached across the table to shake Kevin's hand. "Good to meet you, Kevin," he said. "Do you work here too?"

"Yes. I make the pizza," he said simply, sounding childlike.

Kerri remained silent, but she smiled at him when he glanced her way. He said he had to get back to work, but Lauren insisted on a game of pinball first.

"I have to work," he said as she pulled him toward the video game room.

"You can take a break," she said.

"I just had a break."

"Then take another one. Your dad won't mind."

He went with her but called back to Blake. "Tell Dad I'm on a break."

Blake laughed. "I'll do that, Kevin," he said, but as soon as Kevin had turned his back, Blake simply sat down and told them more about him.

"That's Tony's son. Kevin's been working here since he was ten."

"How old is he now?" Seth asked.

"Twenty-three. And don't let the autism fool you. He's a senior at Humboldt this year."

"He's autistic?" Kerri asked.

"Yes. It's a mild case. Most of his limitations are in the social and communication realm. But he's not short on love or joy. Happy all the time. That's Kevin."

"What's he study at Humboldt?" Seth asked.

"Geography and music. He loves maps. He could get you anyplace in the world. He went to Europe this summer. I'm anxious to hear how that went. He'll be telling us stories about it until Christmas. And he plays the piano—some other instruments too, but that's his favorite. He plays keyboard for the college group on Sunday nights."

"And he really makes the pizzas?"

"Oh, yes," Blake laughed. "If you work here, he'll be training you. He trains everyone new, and if you're not doing it right, he's not afraid to tell you so."

Amber asked Blake if he had talked to Colleen since Thursday. He said he'd talked to her several times and took his phone out to call her right then. Seth and Amber laughed at him, but Kerri's mind was still on Kevin. She had done a report for her *Child Development* class last year on autism, and she had been seriously thinking about going into some kind of field that worked with children with special needs—either from the medical, psychological, or educational side of it. She didn't really know, but that was the clearest kind of direction she had felt thus far, and meeting Kevin on her first full day here made her think God might be trying to confirm that for her in a small way.

But there was also something about him she instantly liked, and she supposed he had that effect on most people. When he returned from playing pinball with Lauren, he briefly gloated to Blake that he had beat her again, but then he waved to all of them and headed for the kitchen.

Kerri got out of her chair and followed him, catching up to him just as he reached the counter area. He turned around to face her when she called out his name, but he didn't appear to recognize her.

"Hi, I'm Kerri. One of Blake's friends."

"Hi, Kerri. It's nice to meet you."

His words sounded rehearsed, like he'd been taught to greet new people with that phrase. He reached out his hand, and she shook it politely. His behavior now was different from the way he had been with Blake and Lauren. More formal and detached.

"I was wondering if you could show me how you make the pizza," she said, suddenly wondering if this was such a good idea. He appeared uncomfortable with her presence.

"Do you want to work here?" he asked.

"No, I just um, I just wanted to watch."

"Watch?"

"Yes. Can I do that?"

"Only people who work here can be in the kitchen."

"Oh, okay," she said, supposing that was a health regulation. "Never mind."

Someone came up behind Kevin at that same moment and put his hand on his shoulder. "We've got orders up, Kev. You coming back now, or should I get them started?"

"No, I'm coming, Dad," he said, beginning to turn away from her.

"Who's this?" his dad asked.

"Who?" Kevin asked as if he'd forgotten about her already.

"This pretty girl here. Is she a friend of yours?"

Kevin looked back at her. "This is Kerri. She's Blake's friend."

Kevin's dad reached out to shake her hand, and she returned the greeting. "Nice to meet you, Kerri. Are you interested in a job here too?"

"No. My brother Seth is. You met him already."

"Oh, sure. We'll probably be seeing more of you then."

"Probably," she said. "I can never turn down good pizza, and I heard Kevin is really good at making them."

"My right-hand man," he said, slapping Kevin on the back. "Would you like to see the pro in action?"

She smiled. "He told me I couldn't be in the kitchen unless I work here."

Tony laughed. "Come on back if you want," he said, tossing her a wink and turning back to face Kevin. "Let's show her how it's done, Kev. New rule: When a beautiful girl wants to see how you make a pizza, the answer is always yes."

Chapter Six

Chad pulled the car into the beach access area and found a parking space. "Does this look okay?" he asked Jessica.

"It looks great," she said, smiling at him sweetly.

Because the traffic was heavy today and they hadn't hit the road construction area Seth had warned him about, he didn't want to stop and go for a walk like she had suggested, but seeing Jessie smile at him that way and recalling the pleasant kiss they had shared two hours ago, he didn't feel like he could tell her no for the world.

He got out of the car and met her on the sidewalk. Taking her hand, he walked beside her toward the stairs that led to the sand below, and he felt glad they had stopped. His legs and back were getting sore from driving, and breathing in the marine air felt good. Being with Jessie in this romantic way rather than sitting beside her in the car had a different feel too. A feeling he liked very much. All of his fears seemed to have vanished with one simple kiss, and he was looking forward to more.

When they hit the sand, Jessie removed her flip-flops and walked barefoot beside him. He released her hand and pulled her close to his side, and she looked up at him and smiled.

"I like us like this," he said, confirming what he had told her earlier.

"I do too," she said. "And now that I know you do, I have something to ask you. You said I could ask you anything today, right?"

"Yes," he replied, not feeling as nervous about that prospect as he had this morning, but not entirely comfortable either, at least not until she spoke the words. There was something about anticipating certain moments with Jessie that scared him, but when they actually became reality he relaxed considerably.

"What do you need most from me in this relationship, Chad? I never feel like I have a clue what guys want except their obvious physical desires, and since I know I can expect better from you, I want to know what those things are."

He thought before he spoke. He knew some things he definitely didn't want because of his experience with Rhonda, but he tried to think of what the opposite of those negative actions and attitudes would be.

"I want you to be honest and real—the way you've been with me so far. I want to know what you want and need from me—in general and on any given day. Like if you've had a long day and need to go do something fun with me, then just say so, or if I'm talking about going into town and doing something and you need to get some studying done instead, then tell me that."

"Like when I wanted to stop and go for a walk on the beach and I told you so. You like that?"

"Yes, and I need you to because my agenda is to get us there as soon as possible, but I needed a break. I need more time with you like this today, but I wouldn't have actually done it on my own."

"Do I talk too much?"

"Is this related to the other question, or a new one?"

"It's related." She laughed. "Do you need me to be more quiet like Amber?"

"I need you to be you. Didn't you just hear me say that?"

"Yes."

"I meant it. I don't want you to be like someone else. If I did, I would have been pursuing them, not you."

"So, you like me for more than the way I look?"

He stopped walking and turned to face her. Taking a good look at her, he knew he had every reason to be attracted to her in a physical way. He'd always thought she had a beautiful appearance, but that wasn't what had kept him interested for over a year. And it wasn't any one thing, it was everything.

He pulled her closer to him and held her, realizing that even with as pretty and confident as she was, she was someone who needed to be loved and cared for. Genuinely. This wasn't just about hanging out together and kissing. This was about them opening their hearts to each other and starting something that could possibly last for the rest of their lives. The thought scared him and thrilled him. And he felt both overwhelmed and confident in the ability of their God to lead them down this unknown path.

Releasing her enough to look into her brown eyes, he met her trusting and curious gaze and kissed her gently. "I like you, Jessica, because I think you might be the woman God has for me."

She appeared to like that answer, and he kissed her again. Knowing that was the honest truth and she was willing to accept it made him feel closer to her, and he knew this open and honest day they were having was working for him.

"What do you need from me, Jessie?"

"Honestly?"

"Yes, honestly," he said, picking her up off the sand and carrying her in his arms. He didn't like having to look down at her all the time, and he wanted this to be a fun day, not just a serious one.

"I don't like to be thrown in the water," she warned him and put her arms around his neck. They were only about ten feet from the shoreline.

"I'm not going to throw you in," he said, turning to walk parallel to the water. "I don't want you getting my seat all wet."

She laughed and leaned into him in a relaxed and trusting way, and he kissed her hair.

"Come on now. Give me your list of demands."

"I want you to be exactly who you are too, Chad. I like it when you're quiet, and I like it when you're like this."

"And what do you need from me? Anything specific? Anything you haven't had before you really wish someone would give you?"

She didn't respond immediately and he carried her away from the water toward some grassy dunes. Putting her down, he sat in the sand and pulled her onto his lap, suddenly feeling like he needed to be the aggressive one in this conversation. He knew she had things to say that were lying deep within her heart or she would have said them already.

He kissed her first, letting her know she could be open and vulnerable with him. "I want to know, Jessie. Tell me, or this isn't going to work, and I definitely want it to work."

She smiled, but it was a cautious smile. He waited for her to speak. When she did, she couldn't look at him directly.

"I'm under the impression you will be this way, but I feel like I need to say it anyway. Don't be mad, okay?"

He waited for her to look at him. When she did, he kissed her forehead and rubbed her back. "I won't be mad."

"I need you to be really strong about—" She stopped and laughed at herself. "Whose idea was this?"

"Yours," he laughed. "And it's a good idea. If we can't be straight with each other, we might as well not bother."

She took a deep breath. "I know."

"What do you need me to be strong about?"

"I need you to be strong about keeping the physical side of our relationship pure. You're a really good kisser, Chad. And you're very gentle and sweet. I could give in to you so fast—" She put her arms around his neck and clung to him. He could tell she was trying to keep from crying, but she didn't succeed.

He held her protectively in his arms and waited for her to speak again. "I don't want to make the same mistakes—" It was all she could choke out.

He closed his eyes and started praying right then, silently pleading with God to never allow him to hurt her in that way—in any way. Ever.

"I will be," he promised her. "I wouldn't be allowing this to happen if I couldn't promise you that."

He held her for a long time, and when she sat back and dried her eyes, he gave her a brief kiss. "You think I'm a good kisser?"

She laughed. "Very good. Too good."

"Well, they're all you get, so you might as well enjoy them."

She didn't respond, and he decided to move on. "Okay, what else? That's a good one, but I know there's more."

She took a moment to think and then said something not quite so serious. "I want you to call me sweetheart."

"Seriously?"

"Yes. I've been called baby and honey and silly pet names, but I want to be your sweetheart."

"And do you prefer Jess, Jessie, or Jessica from me?"

"Either Jessie or Jessica."

"Okay, Jessica, sweetheart. What else?"

She laughed and said something more serious without hesitating this time. "I need you to ask me regularly about my relationship with Jesus. It's easy for me to get lazy about it, but I can't afford to do that. I need my time with Him every day, and for it to be *good* time, not rushed, or I'm a mess."

"I need you to do that for me too. Do you have anything special you're studying right now, or do you want us to do something together?"

"I have a series I'm going through, and it's pretty specific to girls, but we could share with each other what we're doing individually, or if you want to do something together, I could fit that in too. The more I do, the better."

"How about if we wait and see how we're both doing, and if we start to feel like we need to do something together, we can figure it out then."

"Okay," she said. "Just sharing with you might take time to get used to, but I want to. So ask, because I probably won't spontaneously do it."

"Have you had that time today?"

"Yes. This morning, but I was a little tired, so I was planning to go over it again tonight. I usually do that anyway, and it's often not until I get in bed and look back over it that I realize some way God answered a prayer from that morning or I see God in something that happened that day."

"Do you remember anything about it from today?"

She thought for a moment and smiled. "It was about honesty, and at the time I was thinking more about being honest with God, but I'm being pretty honest with you too."

"What were your fears about today?"

"Talking too much and driving you crazy."

"Didn't happen," he said.

"Us not having anything to say to each other and by the end of today knowing it wasn't meant to be."

He smiled. "Thanks to you, that definitely didn't happen."

"It's you too, Chad. You're easy for me to talk to, and I couldn't be around you for more than four hours before I really wanted you to kiss me."

He smiled. "Anything else?"

"I need you to be strong, Chad. But I also need you to make me feel like this."

"Like what?"

"Like you love me," she whispered.

He searched his heart deeply on that one. He knew he had a lot more to learn about this woman. He had learned a lot in the last twenty minutes. He knew what she needed, and he was willing and anxious to give her that. He knew she made him feel things that went beyond physical desire to touching his heart—not an easy place for anyone to get to. And he knew if he was kissing her this way, he'd better have love to go with it, or he was going to get himself in trouble in a hurry.

"I will love you the best way I know how, sweetheart. And I pray it will always be exactly what you need."

*** *** ***

Stepping into the kitchen of Tony's Pizza, Kerri followed Kevin and his dad to the pizza-making area. Tony directed her toward the end of a large counter where she wouldn't be in the way of the others bustling around the kitchen but she could watch Kevin easily. He went straight to work, checking the order slip from where someone had clipped it above the counter, scanning it briefly, and then pulling dough from the refrigerator beside his workspace.

In no time at all he took a ball of dough and slapped it out into a perfect circle, placed it on a pan, pushed the edges out a bit to make it fit, covered it evenly with sauce and then started pulling toppings from the bins. He concentrated completely on what he was doing, never looking at her or anyone else in the kitchen. Even when one of the girls working came over to ask him something, he answered her without looking up from his work.

Once he had the first one done, someone else came to put it into the oven, and he began to work on the next order. She wondered if he remembered she was standing there watching him.

"You're fast," she said, not knowing what else to say except the obvious.

He paused and looked at her, giving her a smile. "I'm good too. The best pizza maker here."

He said it in a prideful, yet non-arrogant way, similar to the way a child would brag about being able to ride a two-wheeler without training wheels.

She smiled. "I'm sure you are. How long have you been doing this?"

"Since four o'clock," he said.

She didn't ask him anything else and let him work. She was fascinated by him. The way he did the same thing every time in the exact same way, and yet acting as if he was doing so for the first time instead of the thousandth. He appeared perfectly happy to be doing it, and to be here. And everyone who interacted with him during the next ten minutes seemed happy he was here too. He didn't bark orders at anyone, and yet if he said something, someone was right there to do exactly as he asked. It was like he was in charge of the kitchen and everyone knew it except him.

"Do you want to try one?" he said, taking the new slip that had just been posted. "This is a small one. Simple. Even you could do it."

"I'd love to. Just tell me what to do."

"You have to wash your hands first," he said, pointing to the sink. "Use soap," he added. "Lots."

She did as she was told, and when she returned, he had the smaller piece of dough waiting for her and a special pan they cooked them in. He actually had to make two of them, so he showed her with his and she copied him, stretching it out a bit and then placing the thick dough the pan. He was quick to point out any detail she didn't do just right, but in a matter-of-fact way, not like he was annoyed she did something wrong.

As a part of the kitchen-staff at camp last summer, she had helped with making pizza before, but this was different from the haphazard way they had assembled them. For Kevin each pizza was a work of art. Perfect. Exact. Just the way he wanted it to be.

Once they had finished the individual-sized pizzas, there was a break in the orders, and she watched as he cleaned up his workspace. "Blake said you went to Europe this summer," she commented.

"Yes, I did."

He didn't add any information, so she tried again. "Where did you go? Which countries?"

"Portugal, Spain, France, Luxembourg, Belgium, Netherlands, Germany, Denmark, Norway, Sweden, Finland, Poland, Czech Republic, Liechtenstein, Austria, Switzerland, Italy, and Greece."

"Is that all of them?"

"No," he said. "We didn't go to England, Ireland, Scotland, Iceland, Slovenia, Hungary—"

She laughed. "Okay, I get it. I'm not great at geography."

He laughed also. It was the first time she'd heard him laugh, and if anything made him sound like he was ten instead of twenty-three, that took the cake.

"That's not all the countries in Europe," he laughed again. "You're silly."

She laughed again, and he laughed harder.

"All right, who let this girl in the kitchen?" Kerri heard Blake say, coming up behind them. "She doesn't work here."

"Dad said it was all right," Kevin said. "She wanted to watch me make the pizzas."

Tony came into the kitchen and posted another order slip on the wall. "Looks like Kerri helped you get caught up, huh, Kev?"

"She made one."

"All right! Maybe we should talk her into working here."

"No," he said, laughing again. "She doesn't know all the countries in Europe. She would never figure out how to make pizzas right."

Tony laughed, and so did Blake and another girl within hearing distance. And then without warning her in any way, Kevin stepped over and gave her a hug.

"I liked you helping me, Kerri. Thanks."

"You're welcome," she said. "I'll let you get back to work now, but maybe I'll come watch again sometime."

"Okay," he said. "My dad says there's a new rule. When a beautiful girl wants to see how I make a pizza, the answer is always yes."

Chapter Seven

"We could go register tomorrow," Matt said. "Unless you have something better to do."

"Does that mean you will stay over tonight?" Mandy asked.

"Yes."

"Sounds great to me," she said, lifting her chin and receiving a sweet kiss.

"Are you sure those are the classes you want to take?"

"Yeah, I think so. Are you sure?"

"We're going to be seeing a lot of each other," he warned.

She smiled. "I suppose I'll deal with it somehow."

They weren't alone in the house. Her mom and dad had left for their Sunday evening Bible study while they had been looking through the community college schedule of classes. But her grandmother was here. She had gone downstairs where she had turned the open basement area into a quilting room, and another woman from the church had come over to help her with their latest project.

Matthew kissed her again, and she sensed a difference in the way he had been kissing her the last few days. It was more intimate than before his brother's accident, but less needy than the turn they had taken that week.

"How are you?" she asked him seriously when he stopped for a moment to look at her.

He smiled. "I'm very good."

"I'm serious, Matthew," she said, receiving another tender kiss. "How are you?"

He seemed to understand what she meant. He hadn't talked about Mark or his family all weekend. "I'm all right. My joy is back."

"And how were things at home last week?"

"Okay. My dad was back at work, and my mom had things to do, so I had a lot of time to myself. I looked through a bunch of pictures, watched some videos, and remembered the good times."

"Why is your joy back?"

"Because you're here. I loved my brother, and I miss him. But I have you, and that helps. God knew I would need you now, and He gave me you at the right time."

"I'm bringing you joy?"

"Yes."

She laughed.

"What?"

"That's ironic because you're the most joy-filled person I've ever met. It was your smile and laugh that kept replaying in my head after I first met you, and I never would have survived this summer if you hadn't been so goofy and adorable on Saturdays."

"I'm most happy when I have something or someone to be happy about. And having you in my life is the best thing that's ever happened to me, Amanda."

"Is that what those kisses are about?"

"Yes."

"I like those."

"In that case," he said, taking the college catalog from her lap and setting it on the coffee table. "I'll have to give you more."

His lips touched hers at the same moment his phone rang. He laughed and reached for it, checking the display to see who was calling him. "Of course. Who else would call me at a time like this?"

He clicked it on and spoke, leaning back against the sofa and pulling her into his chest. "Hey, Seth. How's California?"

***

It was good to hear Matt's voice. "It's all right so far," Seth replied. "How was your weekend?"

"Great. Except for you guys taking off, of course."

"How's Mandy?"

"I think she's all right. She doesn't appear to be sick of me yet."

"Where are you? Is she there?"

"Yes. We're at her house looking through the community college catalog and picking out our classes together."

"Did you tell her about the internship?"

"Yes, at just the right moment. I told you I would."

"I had no doubt about that. I just wondered if it had come yet."

"What are you doing now?"

"We just finished eating, and I thought I'd call you before we head back to the campus. Cell phones don't work too great up there in the forest."

"Have you gotten a new roommate to take my place?"

"We've been gone all afternoon, so I don't know. I'm thinking Chad might be there when we get back, and Adam should be coming soon too. But I wish you were here."

"Me too."

"All right, we won't go there. You're doing the right thing, man. And I admire you for it."

"Thanks. I hope you're right."

"My fiancée is bugging me to talk to Mandy. I guess I'll say bye for now and let them chat. Call me anytime if you need that. I gave you my phone number in the dorm, didn't I?"

"Yep. I'll be using it, I'm sure. And you called at a good time."

"Oh?"

"I'll leave it at that. Don't worry, but pray. I think God is absolutely out of His mind for giving me such a beautiful girl."

"I hear you on that," he said. "Don't forget who has her twin cousin."

Seth passed the phone over to Amber and listened as she talked to Mandy for a few minutes. Silently he prayed for Matt, but he honestly wasn't worried. Matt may be weak when it came to keeping his desires for Mandy in check, but he wasn't short on love for her, and he knew from experience what a difference that could make. His love for Amber outweighed his inappropriate desires, and he knew Matt had the same kind of heart. The mistakes in his past had more to do with looking for satisfaction in places it couldn't be found, not in hurting people. He had a huge heart. He was giving, not selfish. He'd been lost for awhile, but God had found him and brought him home. And Seth trusted God to keep him there.

Once they were back in the car headed for the campus, Seth refocused his attention on Amber, and he had a content and happy feeling to know he would be having time with her this evening, tomorrow, and the day after that. He was excited about signing up for their classes tomorrow and felt hopeful they would have some together this first semester. They would be able to request the classes and times they wanted, and although there was no guarantee they would get it, from what Blake had said, they probably would.

"Do you want to go to your room and have time with Kerri and Lauren?" he asked before they got out of the car.

She smiled at him. "I'll have that later. I'd like more time with you, if that's all right."

He leaned over and kissed her. "Fine with me," he whispered.

She kissed him in return, and he got lost in her touch. Before he knew what was happening, his lips were on her cheek and then her neck, something he wasn't supposed to do in this kind of setting. He pulled away and apologized as soon as his brain caught up with his heart.

She forgave him with a simple smile and suggested they go for a walk. He agreed and got out of the car.

Once they were walking away from the parking area, he apologized again. "That was weird," he said. "I haven't done that before."

She smiled. "I seem to remember you doing that on Friday afternoon," she said, referring to the time they had spent down by the creek at her house.

"I didn't mean that," he said. "I meant my lips getting ahead of my brain."

"I feel it too, Seth."

"Feel what?"

"I'm not sure. But several times today I found myself thinking, 'You could kiss or touch me in any way you want, and I wouldn't care. We're adults now. We're on our own. Let's just enjoy each other.'"

He felt surprised by her admission but knew he had been thinking the same—maybe not consciously, but his actions told him something wasn't right.

"What are we going to do about that?" he asked.

"Pray."

"And what else?"

She stopped walking and turned to face him. "What else is there? We were sitting in the car in broad daylight. If it can happen there, it can happen anywhere."

He closed his eyes and held her close. He prayed silently, beyond words. This was beyond him. Beyond his ability to control. Beyond his own reasoning and logic. Beyond his capacity to restrain his intense feelings of desire for this beautiful and amazing woman.

Slowly he felt new strength taking over his weary soul. New love filling up his heart. And the peace he longed for returned. He hadn't realized he had been missing any of that. He'd lost it yesterday when everything had gone wrong. The stress had gotten to them and done something to their spirits, and only Jesus could restore it.

"Don't let go, Jesus," he prayed for Amber's ears too. "Hang on tight. We need you."

I'm here, Seth. Give it all to Me.

"I feel weak and inadequate. I feel scared to death. What if I can't take care of Amber? What if—"

Give it to Me, Seth.

He resisted the call to surrender. It was too much to hand over. He was supposed to be responsible now. Strong. An adult. Independent.

No, no, no, Seth. You need Me now more than ever. Be My child. Is anything to difficult for Me? Do you suddenly know what's best for you? You think you can do a better job of taking care of Amber than I can?

He sighed and released it all. "She's Yours, Jesus. I'm Yours. Guard us. Teach us. Lead us. You lead, we'll follow."

Now you're talking. There's the Seth I know. Where you been today?

"Show us what to do, Jesus."

Walk over to the housing area for married students. I want to show you something.

Seth released Amber and opened his eyes. She was looking at him with a curious smile. His prayers were usually more structured and flowing than that, and he knew she hadn't heard God's end of the conversation. He prayed that way a lot when he was alone, but not with her—at least not out loud.

He kissed her, and he felt better. He didn't say anything and continued leading them up the path in the direction they had already been heading. The housing for married students was at the other end of the lake from the regular dorms. He had seen the apartments peeking through the trees before but had never been all the way up the path.

"Where are we going?" Amber asked. "You look like you're on a mission."

"Do you know what's up here?" he asked.

She glanced around. "The library?"

She was right about that. The library was ahead of them, but he steered her away as soon as they hit the street. The narrow roadway that came from the main parking area ended in another small parking area adjacent to the apartments.

"This is where we're going to live next year," he said. His heart felt light and alive again, and as soon as they stepped into the courtyard space that was surrounded by quaint and well-maintained apartments, he felt a familiar peace and excitement wash over him.

"Wow, it's nice," she said. "Don't you think?"

He turned to face her and kissed her in a love-filled way. All the anxiety had left him. All the 'what-ifs' were far away. All the thoughts about not knowing what he was doing didn't matter. Jesus had brought them here, and Jesus would carry them. All he had to do was believe that and trust Him every day.

"He loves us, Amber. I don't know much, but I know that. We'll let Him carry us, all right?"

"All right," she smiled.

"I'm glad we're here," he said. "Being with you has always been what I want more than anything."

"Me too, Seth. And you don't have to be any different than you've always been."

Chapter Eight

Amber smiled at Seth and knew her sweet boyfriend was back. All day she had been sensing something wasn't right. He had been more distant than usual—not physically, but emotionally, like he was the one kissing her, but not really.

Several times she'd had an uneasy feeling, but he hadn't done anything to clearly cross the line, so she hadn't said anything. But she had prayed, especially after he'd gotten carried away in the car. She didn't know how to handle Seth's physical need for her when it seemed to be getting away from him.

She could push him away, but he always told her he didn't want her to have to be the strong one. So she had given him over to Jesus during one such moment on the beach this afternoon, and she could see their Savior had broken through and rescued Seth from wherever he'd gone.

Glancing at her surroundings once again, she felt a mixture of excitement and peace about living in this area of the campus with Seth next year. She wondered what the apartments were like inside, but she didn't suppose she could see right now or anytime soon, unless she happened to get to know someone who lived here. But she could wait. Wait to see the inside. Wait to be married to Seth. Wait to see how God led them throughout this year. They were engaged and she felt the difference in their relationship compared to six months ago, but they were still just them. A couple of kids who had fallen in love with Jesus and each other, and neither of them could speculate about what tomorrow would hold.

They crossed the courtyard area and discovered another path leading to the lake, along with a small outdoor swimming pool and a playground that appeared to be for those living in the family housing area. There was another pool outside the gymnasium, along with a weight room, racquetball courts, and a facility with treadmills and other exercise equipment for general use. But the thought of having this area, a more private pool, and spending many hours with Seth here gave her a unique feeling. The same feeling she'd had when she saw God provide the money for her to come here. She knew God had led them here together and He would be faithful to guide them as they navigated their way into adulthood.

They found a place to sit on the grassy bank of the small lake. Seth did kiss her some, but he had gone back to his usual kisses she felt more comfortable with. He explained a bit more how he'd been feeling today and about his prayer that helped him to surrender it all to Jesus. She had felt that way yesterday, but her panicked thoughts had fled once she remembered all God had done to bring them here.

But it had taken Seth longer, and she knew why. He saw her as his responsibility now, and she liked that, but she didn't want him to become overwhelmed by it. Hearing him talk, she knew he had realized his wrong thinking, but she wanted to assure him he had the right perspective now.

"You've already been taking care of me for the past two years, Seth, and I know you've done that by staying close to Jesus and letting Him guide you."

He didn't deny her words. His means of showing her genuine love went beyond kissing and romance to practical needs. She needed to be encouraged in her faith. She needed Seth to keep them from doing the wrong kinds of things. She needed God to guide their decisions about going to camp, college, and getting engaged.

"My dad said something to me before we left yesterday, but I didn't get it until now."

"What?" she asked.

"He said, 'When you think you've got everything under control and everything in order, don't be surprised when God throws it all into chaos.' And at the time I thought he meant God will constantly be challenging me with new things to keep me depending on Him, but now I think he meant whenever I try to handle everything myself, God will show me that's not my job. He will bring me to a point where I say, 'I can't do this,' and He will say, 'Then stop trying.'"

"And let Him do it instead?"

"Yes. I want to take care of you, Amber. But I can't do it by myself. I'm leaving you in God's hands now."

She laughed. "Then you'd better watch out, because He has some pretty crazy ways of doing that."

"I know, and I haven't seen Him fail yet."

***

Lauren enjoyed having time with Kerri while Amber was out with Seth and before Jessica or Adam arrived. Their final week of camp had been crazy and tiring, not giving them much chance to talk other than some brief exchanges. And then she had spent most of her time with Adam on the staff retreat last weekend.

Lauren liked Jessica and Amber and several other girls she had gotten to know at camp this summer, but she could talk to Kerri in a deeper way for some reason, and she hoped in the midst of their busy schedules, sharing this room with two other girls, and her own relationship with Adam, they could find more moments like this. She was happy to see Jessica arrive and help with getting her settled, but their space had been invaded, and she felt that familiar twinge of envy creep into her heart, wishing she was more like Kerri and Jessica who seemed to have all the right clothes and accessories and know-how about being on their own for the first time. They seemed excited and mature. She felt scared to death and clueless.

Adam's arrival an hour later helped to dispel some of that. She wasn't sure he would know how to find her because she wasn't in her original room assignment, but he had gotten the information from Chad and came over as soon as he had dumped his things in his room.

"I couldn't even wait to unpack," he said, kissing her gently in the deserted hallway where she had stepped out to have a private moment with him. "It's good to see you, Angel. I missed you."

"I missed you," she echoed. She had wanted to invite him to go to Shasta Lake with her family last week, but she knew he needed some time with his family before heading off to school, and they would be having plenty of time together once they were here. But it had been a long week.

"Can we go for a walk?" he asked. "Or do you have things you need to do?"

"I'm free," she said.

They took the stairs to the first floor and exited the building. "What's it like having Amber as a roommate?" he asked.

"I'm not sure yet. So far I've only seen her when we went to Tony's for pizza. Have you had dinner?"

"Yeah, but that was awhile ago. Do they have anyplace here we can get something?"

"Yes, at the Oasis," she said. "I think it's open. Do you want to go?"

"Sure."

"What do you have to tell me?" she asked, recalling he had mentioned something when she talked to him on the phone earlier.

"I met your parents today."

"You did?"

"Yep."

"Where? At my house?"

"Yes. When I got to Klamath Falls, I felt like I should meet them before I got down here, so I called and asked if I could drop by. I didn't stay too long, but I let them know they would be seeing a lot more of me in the future."

"And what makes you think that?" she asked with a teasing smile.

He stopped and kissed her. "Because unless you're tired of me already, I'm going to be hanging around."

"I suppose I can deal with that." She smiled and felt herself being tenderly kissed once again.

She realized Adam accepted her simply for who she was. She'd never had to work her way into his affection or be anyone but herself. Just like with her family, Kerri, and a few other close relationships she'd had.

She also realized it wasn't her that made the difference, it was them. She was always the same whether she was with her family, Adam, or around girls she felt intimidated by. But their perception of her made the difference. If they felt drawn to her and liked her for whatever reason, that was up to them. She couldn't change how others saw her.

"I don't want to invade your space too much here, Angel, but I want you to know any time I spend with you will be pure joy for me, and I don't think I can ever have enough. So don't have silly thoughts like, 'I'd really like some time with Adam, but I should let him study or have time with his other friends instead.' If you need me, I'm here, okay? Call me. Drop by. Don't let me out of your sight in the first place."

"Okay," she said. "Thanks for saying that, and for meeting my parents. That means a lot to me."

They continued walking to the center of campus to a place called The Oasis. It was a large student center with comfortable couches, tables for eating and studying, vending machines, and a juice/coffee bar and deli that was open at certain times. Since it was open now, they both got something to drink and nachos to share. Settling themselves at one of the vacant tables, they sat there and talked until they had finished eating and then moved to one of the couches.

She took the poem from her purse she had written earlier and allowed him to read it. He didn't say anything for a moment, but he did pull her close.

"You know what I did this week?"

"What?"

"I prayed a lot. Like five or six times a day about me and you."

She had prayed too, but not quite that much. "What did you pray for?"

"Every night before I went to sleep, I asked God to show me if it was right, and then the next day there would always be something telling me it was. And whenever I thought about different aspects of our relationship, I would pray for that specific area. I asked God for wisdom and for Him to fill up our hearts with love and joy and peace—for each other and for our relationship with Him."

She felt amazed by what he was saying, and she believed he was being sincere. It gave her a safe feeling and reminded her of the way he had been during the last two weeks of the summer.

"One of the confirmations came when my mom asked how long we'd been seeing each other and she told me she had felt led to pray for me more than usual during the last couple of weeks. She didn't know what she was praying for specifically, but she knew there was something going on."

Adam laughed, but his eyes caught sight of something at the same moment, and he stopped.

Lauren followed his gaze across the room and saw two girls walking toward the serving counter. He dropped his eyes but realized he'd already been caught.

"Do you know them?" she asked. They were two very pretty girls, who were dressed too promiscuously in her opinion, and she could imagine every guy in the place looking their way, but she knew Adam hadn't done so just because of that.

"Yes, I do," he admitted.

"Where from?"

"Camp. They were on staff two summers ago—my first year."

"Are you going to say hi?" she asked.

"No, not right now. They might not remember me."

She stared at him curiously. There was something he wasn't telling her.

"In fact, let's go," he said. "I don't want to deal with that right now."

He got up and headed for the nearest door. She followed him and didn't make her inquiry until they were outside and walking back to the dorms.

"Adam? What's going on? Why didn't you want to talk to them?"

"I dated them that summer," he said.

"Both of them?"

"Not at the same time. But yes, both of them."

Chapter Nine

Lauren didn't say anything more about the two girls until they were back at her dorm and riding in the elevator up to the third floor. She realized Adam was likely going to say good-night to her in another minute once they reached her room. He still needed to unpack, and it was getting late. She understood and wouldn't have been bothered by it, except for the way he had obviously been affected by seeing two girls he had dated in the past.

They'd had an honest conversation on their first date about their previous relationships—sort of. Adam had asked if she had ever kissed a guy like she was kissing him, and she told him she hadn't, but not that she hadn't dated before or kissed a guy at all. He hadn't learned that until later in the week.

He hadn't gone into his past relationships much except to say he had never kissed anyone like he was kissing her, and that his dating experience had been very little. Based on what he said that night, she didn't think his relationship with either girl could have been serious or long-lasting. She had a difficult time believing he had lied, but if dating them hadn't been anything significant for him, why was he acting so distant and quiet? Why had he not wanted to talk to them? If they were going to school here, it wasn't like he could avoid them forever.

"What is it, Adam?" she asked. "What aren't you telling me about those girls?"

She could tell by the way he looked at her he was still thinking about it. Whatever had happened, she didn't really care. But she cared about him, and seeing them had upset him. She didn't think him keeping that inside would be the best thing. And because her time was limited, she pressed further when he didn't respond immediately.

"You can tell me anything, Adam. Really. I mean that."

The elevator door opened, and they stepped into the hallway. "Is it all right if I tell you tomorrow?" he asked. "It's kind of a long story."

"Can you wait that long?" she asked. "Sometimes things seem bigger when I let thoughts swim around in my mind—especially overnight. Telling someone usually helps."

He didn't respond, and she allowed him to think about it until they reached the end of the hall. She knew he probably wouldn't want to talk here, and she was willing to go for another walk or find a quiet corner in the lounge downstairs.

"I know I can talk to you, Angel, and I'm not hiding anything from you, honest. I've told you this is the first relationship I've had that means something special to me, and I wasn't lying about that. My relationships with Abby and Elissa were both short and meaningless. In fact, I mostly forgot about them after the summer, but seeing them now makes me realize some of what I went through is still there, you know?"

She did know. She often experienced that concerning the loss of her little brother. She would go for months thinking it was all behind her, and then something would trigger a memory, and all those emotions would be right there again.

"I'll tell you tomorrow," he said. "I need to unpack and get some rest."

"Okay," she said, respecting his wishes to keep it to himself for now.

He pulled her close to him. "Thanks for caring," he said.

She opened the door and planned to say good-night to him, but her roommates were all there and saw Adam in the doorway. Kerri came over to give him a hug and invited him in for a minute. He seemed shy about being the only guy in the room, and Lauren could imagine why. He had liked both Kerri and Amber, and she wouldn't be surprised if he'd had his eye on Jessica at some point too. They treated him sweetly, and it was obvious they all liked him in a friendship way and liked seeing them together.

"Your fiancé wasn't in the room when I was earlier," Adam said to Amber. "Should I expect him to be there now?"

"Yes, I think so. He was on his way there ten minutes ago."

He only stayed for a minute and gave her a kiss before politely excusing himself. Lauren closed the door and turned back to find three sets of eyes on her.

She smiled. "What?"

"You two are adorable," Kerri said.

She felt a little embarrassed but mostly thrilled her roommates seemed to think they were a perfect match. "Yeah, I kind of like him," she said.

***

Once outside in the cool evening air, Adam walked toward the guys' dorms on the other side of the parking area, but instead of stopping there and going up to his room, he took the path that led to the prayer chapel. He hadn't been there before, but he followed the sign and saw the quaint structure come into view around the backside of one of the main campus buildings. It was sitting in the middle of a grassy area surrounded by nice landscaping, and the serene setting calmed him even before he stepped through the front door.

It was empty, as he was hoping. He walked toward the front and sat on one of the benches, placed his elbows on his knees, and bowed his head. He felt the need to pray, but he wasn't sure how, and he sat there for a minute, collecting his thoughts. As he'd told Lauren, his relationships with Abby and Elissa had been short and hadn't meant much to him at the time, but significant things had happened that summer.

He'd met them both on the first day of camp. They were best friends who had come together to work on the crew team, and initially he'd been more attracted to Abby but worked with Elissa a lot during the first couple of weeks. He ended up going on a date with Elissa on the third weekend, although that hadn't been his intention.

Abby had to go home for a family reunion, and Elissa mentioned to him while they were working in the kitchen together that she was debating about going home too or just spending Saturday at the camp. He'd said something like, 'If you stay here, maybe we could go do something,' but she had taken it wrong.

It didn't take him long to figure out she really liked him and considered the afternoon and early evening they spent together to be a date. He decided he wouldn't be totally opposed to the idea, and the following weekend when his friend Warner decided to ask Abby out, the four of them went to the beach together on a double date, but he'd had a really lousy time.

He liked being with Elissa on an individual basis, but when she was with Abby, she acted totally different. He'd endured the day—even Warner was getting on his nerves with the way he acted around Abby. He knew Elissa wanted him to kiss her when they went on a walk on the beach together and Warner and Abby had gone in the opposite direction, but he didn't want to, and so he hadn't.

He wanted to tell her he just wanted to be friends, but he didn't know how. When they didn't work together the following week, he made no effort to have any contact with her. She cornered him near the end of the week to ask why he was avoiding her, and he told her the truth, but it didn't go well—not well at all. She ended up having to talk to her senior counselor about it because she felt so hurt, and then Blake had come to talk to him to find out what had happened.

Blake hadn't been too hard on him. He had been through a difficult breakup himself a couple of months before the summer, so they had a good talk about being honest with girls instead of letting them assume things that weren't true, and then by Saturday morning before they finished out the week, Elissa had come to him and said she forgave him.

A couple of weeks later he was assigned to work with Abby in the Snack Shack during Family Camp while Elissa was home for their mid-summer break. After two days of working so closely with Abby and having time with her in the evenings also, his original attraction for her had returned in full force. She had been really nice to him, acting as if nothing had happened between him and Elissa, and when she asked if he could give her a ride home on his way to Bend, instead of having to borrow Elissa's car and drive through the mountains all by herself, he agreed.

He treated it as a friendship-thing initially, but unlike with Elissa, he wanted it to be more than that, and when he arrived at her house to drop her off, he walked her to the door, discussed when he would be picking her up in two days, and then in an uncharacteristic bold moment, he kissed her.

It was simple and gentle, but she seemed to enjoy it, and he did also. He told her he would call her the next day, and he did, and she seemed happy about that. He asked her directly if she had a problem with them dating since Elissa was her best friend, and she said she was fine with it and thought Elissa would be too.

He had an uneasy feeling about it, but he justified his actions because he had never really liked Elissa as more than a friend in the first place and she had misunderstood his intentions. He had originally liked Abby anyway, so he didn't feel like he was doing anything wrong, but he hadn't taken the time to ask God His opinion on the matter. Now he knew he would have heard God telling him no, not necessarily because of what had happened with Elissa, but because He knew what would be coming.

He picked Abby up for the drive back to camp, and they stopped to get dinner on the way. He kissed her in the car before they continued driving, similar to the way he had kissed her before—only several times instead of just once. Then that week they had written sweet notes to each other, talked whenever they had the chance, and he thought about her at all hours of the day.

On Saturday they went to the reservoir, just the two of them, and he was having a genuinely good time until she lured him into a secluded location, asked him to kiss her, and then became sexy and suggestive with her words and her touch, taking him completely off-guard and making it very difficult for him to be a good Christian boy.

He hadn't allowed anything to happen, even when she pouted and begged him to touch her. His relationship with God then hadn't been very strong, but strong enough for him to know it wasn't right and he couldn't go there. He tried to downplay it at first, thinking he could still have her as his girlfriend and stick to his convictions, but by the time they parted that evening, he knew he wasn't going to be able to handle it for long.

Talking to Blake about it the following day, he asked for his prayers and advice and hadn't argued when Blake said, 'Get out now, Adam. Run for your life and don't look back. That's not the kind of girl you're looking for no matter what your eyes may be telling you.'

He had taken Blake's advice and broke up with her that evening. She'd done the same thing Elissa had, going to her senior counselor and acting like the innocent victim of an insensitive, flaky boyfriend who made her think things that weren't true. He was glad he'd gone to Blake first because he had the support of his own senior counselor behind him to let others know there was more to the story, although neither he nor Blake ever told anyone else what those specific things were.

He spent the remainder of the summer avoiding both Elissa and Abby as much as possible, and he had mostly put it behind him and forgotten about it once he went home and got back to his regular life. But the whole experience had made him realize he needed to take spending time with girls more seriously, not be flippant about it and allow them to assume things that weren't true. And it also made him be more selective and to wait until he knew a girl well before asking her out, and not kissing her unless he knew it was right.

Knowing he couldn't avoid Elissa and Abby here indefinitely, his stomach turned at the thought of having one or both of them in any of his classes. He felt confused as to why God would have them here. By the way they were dressed today, he wasn't too optimistic they had changed much. He said a prayer for any guys who encountered them, and he asked for peace to keep his focus on God, Lauren, and his classes, not be distracted by their presence.

He prayed for Lauren also. He needed to tell her everything, and if she had any classes with either Elissa or Abby, that could be awkward and unsettling for her too. Even knowing they were here could have that effect, and he didn't want her feeling any less of herself than the way he saw her. She was beautiful and wonderful, and he wanted her to know that, believe it, and live like it every day.

Chapter Ten

"How did your day with Jessica turn out?" Seth asked.

Chad looked up from the dresser where he was placing his clothes and smiled. "I think it turned out rather well."

"How well?"

Chad was neither surprised nor threatened by Seth's curiosity. He was glad Seth brought up the subject because he wanted to talk about it but would have been too shy to say it on his own.

"I kissed her finally," he said. "And then we had a very honest talk about what we both want and need from this relationship."

"Feel like sharing, or is that none of my business?"

"I need it to be your business so you can hold me to it."

"I'm happy to do that."

Chad finished putting his shirts away and sat on the edge of the bed facing Seth, who had taken a seat on Adam's currently bare mattress. Seth would be sleeping on the other side of the two-room suite and share the space with their fourth roommate. No one had arrived yet, and Seth didn't know if someone would be assigned to this room in Matt's place, but for now he was assuming it.

"She needs me to be strong about the physical side of things, and I want to be, but I know it won't be easy."

"But not impossible. Two years with Amber has proved that to me."

"She wants me to keep her accountable spiritually, and I asked her to do the same in return. How have you and Amber best accomplished that?"

"I've mostly looked at it from the perspective that if I have any hope of having a healthy relationship with Amber—physically and emotionally, then I need to be healthy spiritually. That motivates me to stay close to God, and I just share with her what I'm learning, which seems to have motivated her to have things of her own to share. It's not like I've had to keep after her about it or she's had to keep reminding me. We've done it together. It's a huge part of our relationship that once we started we couldn't be the same without."

"My time with God has always been very personal and not something I go around sharing with everyone," he admitted. "Letting Jessica into that part of me won't be easy."

"It will be easier than you think. Don't be afraid of it. I remember when I decided to give Amber that purity bracelet on her birthday, I felt like there was no way I could say what I wanted to say. I barely knew her, but once I started talking, it was like the most natural thing in the world. I think things are just easy with the right person."

"So, if I can't talk to her, she might not be the right one for me?"

"She might be, but you might need to take things slow until you feel more comfortable. And in my opinion, if you can't share what's on your heart, then you shouldn't be sharing your lips with her either."

Chad knew they hadn't had trouble with either kissing or talking today, so Seth was probably right.

"In fact, now that I say it, I know that's the mistake I made today," Seth said.

"What mistake?"

"After what happened yesterday, I was having stupid thoughts about whether Amber and I should be engaged and if I can take care of her like I want to, but instead of talking to her about it and sharing all my insecurities, I tried to hide them behind a bunch of kisses that nearly got me into trouble."

Chad knew that's what he had let happen with Rhonda. He'd been so insecure about dating her, but physically she seemed to like what he did, so he let that make up for his lack of words and connecting with her emotionally, and she hadn't tried to stop him. They were having sex, but they barely knew each other. It seemed unbelievable now, but at the time it's all he'd known to do.

They were interrupted by Adam opening the door and coming into the room. He'd been anxious to see Lauren when he arrived earlier, but now he appeared subdued. Seth hadn't been here, so he didn't seem to notice, but Chad said what he was thinking.

"You all right, man?"

Adam sighed. "Do you ever have moments where you think, 'God, what in the heck are you doing?'"

"What happened?"

"I was having a perfectly good time with Lauren. She was happy to see me, and I was happy to see her. And then we're sitting over at The Oasis talking and finishing our smoothies, and in walk two girls I dated a couple of years ago that I'd rather forget about. Why God? Why here? Why now?"

"Did you talk to them?"

"No."

"Does Lauren know?"

"Yes, but I didn't tell her the whole story. I managed to put that thrilling task off until tomorrow."

"You should tell her now," Seth said. "Go call her. You can use my landline if you want some privacy. The number is right by the phone."

"I'll tell her tomorrow."

Chad exchanged glances with Seth. "Now, Adam. You'll feel better."

Adam took their advice and went to the sleeping area on the other side of the room, closing the sliding door behind him. Seth laughed, and Chad knew he was laughing at him, not Adam.

"What?"

"Jessie is good for you."

Chad knew he had spoken to Adam from experience. He'd had so much anxiety about today, but talking with Jessica had lessened it significantly. He had a spontaneous thought, and he went with it. He hadn't talked to her since leaving her to unpack, and he hadn't planned on seeing her any more today, but he wanted to know how she was doing.

He decided to run over to the dorm and check on her in person. On his way he felt a little uncomfortable about dropping in, but he knew he wanted to, and the promise he had made to Jessie today was to always be honest. The curfew time for guys being out of the girls' dorms was ten o'clock, and it was just past nine-thirty, so he wouldn't have much time, but even a few minutes would be nice.

Kerri answered the door when he arrived, and she smiled at him. "Well, Mr. Williams. What brings you to our door?"

"I'm here to see Miss Jessica. Is she here?"

Kerri laughed. "Yes."

Jessica appeared in the doorway then, and she smiled.

"Can I talk to you for a minute?" he asked.

She stepped into the hallway and closed the door. Her happy expression had turned to one of curiosity and concern. "You okay?"

He smiled and pulled her close to him, kissing her softly, absolutely loving the fact he could do that. "I was just missing you a little."

He kissed her again, and it felt good. Not just physically speaking, but for his heart. It had been a long day. Having a few more kisses and some time with her wasn't just nice. He needed it.

"Are you still okay with this, or are you having second thoughts?"

"No second thoughts," she said easily. "I loved everything about our time together today, Chad, and I want more of the same—if you do too."

"I do," he said, realizing five minutes with her in the hallway wasn't going to be enough. "Go for a walk with me?"

She smiled. "Let me grab a jacket."

She disappeared inside for a moment, and when she returned she had on a light blue hoodie and jeans. It reminded him of the way she had often dressed at camp in the evenings and how he'd admired her from a distance. She was beautiful, and he wondered how many other guys on this campus would think so too, and how he could possibly hang on to her for himself.

***

Lauren listened as Adam explained about Elissa and Abby, feeling glad he had called so she wouldn't be up wondering about it tonight, and for Adam's sake too. She didn't feel she needed to know the details as much as he needed to share them. The part that told her the most was how he had escaped serious temptation with Abby, and she knew he couldn't be lying because he had talked to Blake about it two years before she ever knew him.

"How did you say no to that?" she asked. "I'm sure it's one thing to not touch me because you know I don't want you to, but something completely different when a girl is so willing to let you do whatever you want."

"I just knew it wasn't right. I'm sorry, Lauren. I'm sorry they're here. I—"

"It's not your fault, Adam. Don't worry about it. I won't."

"You won't?"

"No. Why should I? Are you planning to break up with me so you can go through that with them all over again?"

"No."

"You didn't do anything wrong, Adam. And if it becomes a problem in some way, we'll deal with it then, okay?"

"Okay."

"If something happens with one of them, don't hide it from me. You don't have to do that."

He sighed and admitted his thoughts. "My main fear is that you will think those are the kind of girls I'm really interested in, but I'm not, Angel. You're the one I want. Believe that, okay? I've finally found you, and I don't want to lose you."

"I'm not going anywhere."

"Will you meet me for breakfast?"

"Yes. What time?"

"Anytime you want."

"Are you sure about that?"

He laughed. "Okay, anytime after eight."

"We have an orientation meeting at nine, so how about eight-thirty?"

"That's fine."

"I was thinking about something I forgot to ask you before," she said.

"What?"

"When we were at Tony's earlier, he was asking me if I wanted to work there, and I was thinking maybe we both could and get the same hours. Are you interested in that?"

"Sure."

"Okay, maybe we can find time to go down there tomorrow and fill out applications."

"Sounds good to me," he said. "Can I have the whole day with you?"

"Yes."

"I want to be with you, Angel. Don't forget that, okay?"

"You make that pretty difficult."

"But don't stop reminding you?"

"Yes, I need to hear it."

"I'm glad we're here together. It will give me lots of chances to say it and show it."

She didn't get a chance to respond before he spoke again.

"Oh, it looks like our other roommate is here, and since I'm sitting on his bed, I'd better go."

"Okay. See you tomorrow then."

"Bye, Angel. I can't wait."

Chapter Eleven

Josiah Eastman set his bags on the floor and reached out to shake the hand of another one of his roommates. He had already met Seth, and Seth introduced them.

"This is Adam. Adam, this is Josiah."

"Hey, Josiah. Good to meet you."

"Good to meet you," he replied.

"You're getting here late. Where are you from?"

"Bellingham, Washington. It's a bit of a drive."

"Did you come by yourself?"

"Yep. I don't know a soul here, and I just decided to come last weekend."

"Now you know us, and this guy right here," Adam said, slapping Seth on the back, "is the best roommate you could have gotten, so no worries."

Josiah hoped that was true, and he assumed it was. Seth had already been welcoming and friendly. "Did you two know each other before coming here?"

"Yes," Seth said. "We've worked together at camp the last two summers."

"What camp?"

"Camp Laughing Water, in Oregon."

"I've been there," he said, feeling better about this by the second. He wasn't big on new places and experiences. God had practically dragged him down here. He had lived in Bellingham his whole life. Same church, same school, same neighborhood.

"When were you there?" Seth asked.

"Last summer. My best friend was living with his grandparents somewhere near there while his mom and dad were on a short-term mission trip, and they signed him up to go, so he invited me to come down and go with him."

"Who was your counselor?"

"Shark."

"That's wild," Seth said. "He's my girlfriend's brother."

"No way."

"Yep. It sounds like God destined us to be roommates. My best friend was supposed to be here, but it didn't work out."

"Hey, what are me and Chad?" Adam said. "Not your best friends?"

Seth laughed. "Okay, another one of my best friends was supposed to be here—"

"Nope, too late. I'm offended. Chad too. Right, Chad?" Adam said, stepping out of the sleeping area to his own side.

"He's not here," Seth called after him.

"Where did he go?"

"To see Jess."

"Oh, brother. Already?"

"Yeah right. Look who's talking."

Seth laughed, and Josiah could tell this was probably going to be all right. He didn't tell Seth so, but he and his best friend—the same one he had gone to camp with—had a bit of a falling out this summer. Gabe had done some things he didn't agree with, and their plans to attend college in Seattle together and be roommates had come to an abrupt halt.

He could use strong Christian guys around him right now. Guys who knew God as Someone more than who they learned about on Sunday. Gabe had been pretty strong last summer, but he had taken a major fall this year, and Josiah had tried to talk to him several times but knew he had failed. He was tired of being the strong one and needed others to be that for him right now.

Seth kept talking to him while he unpacked, asking him about his family and interests and what had led him here at such a late date. He felt comfortable sharing with him. Seth seemed like a good guy, and he was a youth ministry major too, confirming God must have destined for them to be roommates and someone he could count on to be a good friend.

"So, that's my story," he said, sharing a brief version of how he had decided not to go to Seattle Pacific with Gabe when his youth pastor had recommended Lifegate instead. "How about you?" he asked.

"God led me and Amber here last November, so we've known for awhile, but it was a fast decision process for us too."

"Who's Amber?"

"My girlfriend—or rather, fiancée. The love of my life."

Josiah smiled. Now he was sounding like Gabe, only Seth was marrying the love of his life, not losing her over some cheap relationship with another girl. He could imagine Gabe and Rachael getting married too if he hadn't blown the best thing that had ever happened to him.

"Good for you, man," he said. "When's the wedding?"

"Next summer."

"Will you be going here next year too?"

"That's what we're planning," he said. "I suppose God could change that, but somehow I doubt it."

"And your family? Do you have brothers and sisters?"

"Two brothers and two sisters. Kerri is here."

"Older?"

"We're twins. She's rooming with Amber. You can meet her tomorrow."

***

"I don't know about you, but I'm ready for bed," Mandy said. She didn't think she could keep her eyes open for another second. Her mom and dad had returned from Bible study and gone to bed along with her grandmother an hour ago.

"Sounds good to me," Matt whispered. "Let's go."

She shook her head and smiled, rising to her feet and pulling him with her. "What would you say if I actually said, 'Okay'?"

"And what would you say if I actually followed you to your room?"

"I don't believe you would ever do any such thing, Matthew Abramson."

He kissed her one last time. "You're right. I just like to tease. You know that."

"I know," she said.

"Good night, baby. I love you."

Mandy left him standing there beside the couch where he would be sleeping, and she went to the bathroom first to brush her teeth and then went to her room at the end of the hall. Once inside the private space, she got into her pajamas and took out her journal to read what she had written earlier in the day. She had gotten into the habit of doing that this summer, ending the day with the thoughts she started it with.

This morning she and Matt had read some verses together, shared their thoughts, and she had written things about how the words applied to her specifically, followed by a prayer.

You have made known to me the path of life; you will fill me with joy in your presence, with eternal pleasures at your right hand. Psalm 16:11

The path I most need to be on is the one that leads me into God's presence. This is where I will find joy and pleasures that will last. It doesn't matter what school I go to, or what classes I take, or what career I choose, or whom I marry, or where I live, or even what I do for God if I am not on the path that leads to Him. He Himself should be my goal. To know Him. To love Him. To experience *Him* for who *He* truly is. *And* if *I* have joy, then *I* know *I'm* on my way there. *If I* don't, *I'm* going the wrong way.

I have so much joy right now *Jesus, I* know *I* have to be doing something right. *Going* to community college was certainly not in my plans——ever. *But* after looking at the classes with *Matthew* last night, *I* feel so excited. *I* wasn't this excited about going to *Lifegate* with him! *How* can that be?

As we look more seriously and pick specific classes, *I* ask that you would guide us. *Thank* you for providing a good job for *Matthew*——something *I* know he will enjoy and will be so worthwhile. *I* know it will limit our time together on the weekends, so help me to handle that. *And* help *Matthew* to continue to deal with his grief properly and with his relationship with his mom and dad. *Help* me not to be resentful toward them and to show them as much genuine love as *I* can, love that *I* know can only come from you.

When I'm with you, *I* know *I'm* all right, no matter what. *So* keep me there. *Keep Matthew* there. *And* help his parents to find their way there.

She didn't fully remember writing all of that, and yet she knew her joy had only increased as the day went on. Her time with Matthew had been pure joy. Choosing their classes had gone well and had been easier than she thought it would be. Hearing from Amber had been good too. She missed her already, and yet she knew Amber and Seth were in the right place for them.

Amber had shared briefly about their difficult day yesterday, but Mandy heard that familiar peace and joy in her cousin's voice, telling her she would be fine. She did take a moment to pray for her and Seth and the others who were there. She also prayed for her family and her friends from camp, and then she turned out her light and went to sleep.

In the morning after breakfast, she and Matthew had their Bible-reading time together once again and then they went to the college to register for their classes. They could have done it online, but they wanted to tour the campus and get out of the house. The lines were short, so it didn't take them any extra time, and they grabbed lunch there too and then decided to drive to Multnomah Falls, a tourist attraction about twenty minutes from the school. They hiked all the way to the top on a well-maintained trail that was only a mile long but was uphill all the way, so it took serious effort. Matthew gave her a piggyback ride part of the way. He could take longer strides with each step and had been a serious athlete in high school, but even he said it was a tough workout.

But it was worth it. At the top was a gentle flowing stream that wasn't wide or deep, and it was amazing to think the spectacular sight of a 600 foot waterfall could come from something so simple and ordinary as a small mountain stream.

They sat up there for a long time, dangling their toes in the water and talking as other tourists came and went. A few times they were alone enough to share extended kisses, but just being with Matthew had its own appeal too, especially when he got insightful and shared something romantic that nearly made her cry.

"You're like this stream, Amanda," he said. "All quiet and unassuming, just weaving your way through life wherever it takes you. And I'm like that waterfall—flashy and loud, attracting a crowd, and out of control sometimes. But we fit together. We can be one-and-the-same despite our differences."

She gave him a sweet kiss. "And that waterfall definitely needs this stream or it would be nothing."

He laughed. "You've got that right."

"I'm just teasing. You're something pretty great with or without me."

"But I prefer to have you," he said. "And I do need you. I know it's hard for you to see, but I do. When I'm with you, everything's just better. Do you know the only thing that God said was not good during the week of Creation?"

"What?"

"It is not good for man to be alone."

She smiled. "Who told you that?"

"It's in the Bible."

"I know, but who pointed it out to you?"

"One guess."

"Seth?"

"Yes, right before I broke up with Clarissa. He said, 'God said it's not good for man to be alone, but He also said He would make someone suitable for him. He has someone for you, Matt. Someone that's right. Wait for her.' And so I did, but those months of waiting were tough. I don't like being alone, or in a crowd when I don't have at least one person I feel really connected to. But when I'm with you, I always have that, and it changes everything."

"Even when we weren't together this summer?"

"We were always together. I couldn't always see you or hold you, but you were there."

***

Jessica knew it had to be getting late. She and Chad had walked around for at least an hour before sitting down in the amphitheater outside the library where they had been talking more, and kissing.

"What time is it?" she asked. The college didn't have an official curfew time they were supposed to be in their dorms, but she had made a personal commitment to never be out past midnight alone with Chad, and she didn't think it would be good to break it on their first day.

"Eleven-thirty," he said. "I should probably walk you back, huh?"

"Yes," she said, knowing that would be wise. She didn't think Chad was crossing the line with his kissing, but his touch was appealing to her, and she wanted more, but she couldn't have it. At this rate she would be sleeping with him by October.

He stood to his feet and pulled her up. They ascended the steps to the top and walked down the paved path to the street. Neither of them said anything until they had reached the door to Priscilla Hall, her new home. Chad couldn't come inside the building this late.

"Thanks for a great day, Chad," she said, accepting his warm embrace and hugging him in return. "You took good care of me."

"I hope I don't ever fail you, sweetheart."

"Let's try hard not to fail each other. I think God brought us together at the right place at the right time, don't you?"

"Yes," he said.

Jessie used her key to open the outside door and stepped inside, waving at Chad as she turned away. She headed for the stairs and walked to her room. Entering quietly, she saw Kerri was in bed, but she wasn't asleep.

"That was some walk," she whispered.

Jessica sat on the edge of her bed and removed her shoes. "I can't believe this is happening, Kerri."

"What's happening?"

"I'm falling in love."

"For real?"

"For real. Chad is so—" She couldn't think of the right word.

"Sweet?"

"Yes, but it's more than that. Everything I said I wanted out of this relationship, he's giving to me, but it's not like he has to force himself. He's trying so hard and not trying at the same time."

"And what have you been doing for the past two hours?"

"Talking and kissing."

Kerri smiled. "A lot of kissing?"

"Not a lot. Well, yes," she laughed. "But not too much. I can enjoy it without having to worry about what he's going to try next."

"And you think it's going to stay that way?"

"Yes, I do, and you know why?"

"Why?"

"Because that's what I've asked God for."

***

Jessica went to use the bathroom, and Kerri knew Jess was right about Chad being an answer to her prayers. She said a prayer for both of them while she waited for Jessica to return, and she was reminded she had asked God for specific things regarding her first semester of college, but she had been lying here for the past half-hour worrying about it all instead of believing God would guide her in choosing the right classes, a major, and the best ways to make use of her time. She was debating about getting a job, and she also wanted to get involved in the right ministry, but she wasn't sure what.

Okay, God. Help me to have peace like Jess does that you're going to answer my prayers and I don't need to worry or try to figure it all out for myself. I know that's how Seth and Amber have been living, and it's working for them. Help me to be that way too.

In the morning she felt more at peace about the first day of orientation, and throughout the week she maintained that. She was eligible for on-campus work-study, and she got her first choice of working at The Oasis. She wanted to work there because she knew it would be a good place to meet a wide variety of people, and she found that to be true in the weeks that followed.

She usually worked on Sunday evenings, Tuesday and Wednesday afternoons until six, and then on Friday evenings. Most people didn't want to work then, but she actually liked it best because it stayed busy the whole time. She remained undecided about her major for now. It didn't really matter yet because she had lots of general classes to take, but she didn't like the feeling of not knowing where she was headed, especially when people asked her, but she kept telling herself it was okay. Some of her friends, including Amber and Lauren, were still undecided too, so that helped.

She liked her classes okay, and all of her teachers were nice, but the highlight of her college experience was all the new friends she was making. She encountered a few people she didn't care for, but mostly everyone was friendly, and the guys who were a little too friendly seemed to respect it when she would say she wasn't interested in dating anyone right now, which she had decided to continue to say until there was someone she really wanted to take a chance with.

Seth's new roommate was nice, she thought, and Seth had a lot of good things to say about Josiah, but so far he hadn't done anything to indicate he was interested in dating her, so she kept it friendly and light also. The only thing she liked better than meeting new people and getting to know them was hanging out with the great friends she already had, especially all three of her roommates. She had individual time with each of them in different ways. She had classes with both Lauren and Amber, and she and Jess spent lots of time talking when they were both in the room studying. And she also had special times with Amber and Seth every Tuesday and Thursday morning following the Old Testament class they had together.

During the first week, Amber and Seth decided to have their Bible-reading time together then on those days, and they had asked her to join them. It didn't take her long to see why her brother and his fiancée had such a strong spiritual relationship. They talked about God, dug into His Word, and prayed together like she rarely heard any two people do outside of church. It was similar to her own personal times with God, but with all three of them sharing their thoughts and the ways it related to their current lives, it became the highlight of her week.

She made a special point to thank them for including her in their time one day in late September when she shared personal things with them about how she was struggling in her faith and walk with God right now.

"You two are so special to me," she said, wiping her tears away. "I thought coming here was about me coming to a great school, but I think it's really about me being here with you. You can't imagine how much I need this right now."

"We're here, Kerri," Seth said, giving her a long hug. "For whatever you need, anytime. Not just for the time we do this."

"I know. And most of the time I can go to God and He gives me what I need, but having this time with you—I feel like it's a special gift He's giving to me right now when I really need it."

Chapter Twelve

Amber enjoyed her first month of college. She liked most of her classes and had at least one person she had known before coming here in each of them: Jessica in *English Composition*; Lauren in her general conditioning P.E. class; psychology with Kerri, and both of her Bible classes, *Old Testament Survey* and *John's Writings*, with Seth. Studying about the Apostle John's life, ministry, and unique writings was her favorite thing academic-wise, both in the classroom and studying outside of class. Her other classes were okay, but that was the one she always looked forward to.

Her time with Seth was great also. He started working at Tony's, and he usually worked on Sunday, Tuesday, and Thursday evenings. Tuesday and Thursday were the days she had classes with him, and they studied together on the other evenings and saw each other on Friday and Saturdays too. She saw him every day, and while she enjoyed a lot of aspects of college life, that was the best.

She also enjoyed getting to know Lauren and rooming with her. They were a lot alike except Lauren was a morning person and tended to go to bed by nine-thirty, while she herself usually finished up with her studying about then and liked to stay up for another hour or two writing on her stories. The first couple of weeks had been an adjustment to have a roommate and needing to think about being quiet once Lauren was in bed and then being awakened earlier than she needed to get up.

But on Tuesday of the fifth week of classes, she never heard Lauren get up at six a.m., nor her other roommates around seven-thirty, and she woke up to a quiet dorm room at eight forty-five, fifteen minutes before her Old Testament class at nine. Knowing she would never get there in time, she decided to skip the lecture today. She could get the notes from Seth later.

After getting up and taking a shower, she went to get breakfast. Entering the dining hall, she got a tray and made her selections and then turned to find a seat. Spotting a familiar face, she went to sit with Adam, whom she hadn't seen a lot of other than when Lauren was with him. They didn't have any classes together, and she didn't know much about his schedule except he had one class with Lauren and he worked in food service, so Lauren often ate whenever he could.

"Hey, what are you doing here today?" he asked.

"I overslept," she said.

"What class are you missing right now?"

"Old Testament. But I have it with Seth, so I'll borrow his notes. What about you?"

"I have Western Civ at ten-thirty, so I work breakfast on Tuesdays and Thursdays."

"Have you seen Lauren already today?"

"No. I can't usually get a break until now, and she has a class at eight."

"And you don't meet her before you have to be here?" she teased him. She knew Adam wasn't any more of a morning person than she was.

"I don't know how you ever did that with Seth at camp. I tried it our first week here, but my mind is mush at that time of the morning."

"I think it was because I knew if I didn't have that time with him, I wouldn't for the rest of the day. It's not that way here, so I'm not getting up at six a.m. either."

"How did we both end up with morning people? I should let Lauren have Seth, and I'll take you."

She laughed. "But you love her anyway, huh?"

He smiled. "You've got that right."

***

Seth wasn't too worried about Amber not meeting him for breakfast or showing up for class, but he was relieved to see her waiting for him outside the building when he descended the front steps of Chambers Hall with Kerri.

"There she is," he said, giving her a brief kiss before demanding an explanation. "Where were you? I was worried."

"Sorry," she said. "I overslept."

"I didn't know if I should wake you before I left or not," Kerri said. "You're usually out of there before me, so I thought maybe you weren't feeling well."

"It's fine," she said. "I suppose I needed the extra sleep."

"Were you up late writing again?" Seth asked, pulling her close to him as they walked toward the outdoor amphitheater where they usually went at this time.

"Yes," she said. "I was at a really good part, and I couldn't stop."

"How late?" he asked.

"You'll be mad."

"No, I won't. I think you should write as much as you want to."

"Two-thirty."

"Two-thirty!"

She laughed. "I looked at the clock at one and thought, 'Okay, I'll just finish this scene,' and then the next time I looked it was two-thirty."

He tickled her, but he didn't take back his word about not being mad. "And what story are you working on that is so compelling?"

"Matt and Mandy's. I'm almost finished."

"That's great, sweetheart," he said, giving her a kiss on the cheek. "I'm proud of you."

"Thanks," she said, seeming to appreciate his support. He wanted to give her as much as she needed because he really believed she had a gift and she should take it wherever God led her.

He enjoyed their Bible-reading time together like always, and having Kerri join them was nice too. He had asked Amber if she minded, and she said she didn't. She seemed to enjoy hearing Kerri's perspective on things and was genuinely concerned about Kerri's confusion and uncertainty about her future. Seth wasn't sure what that was about. Kerri had never been too concerned about it in the past.

She could do anything she wanted, in his mind, but she seemed unsettled since being here, and he didn't know if it was really about school or something of a personal nature.

On Wednesdays and Fridays they were supposed to attend Chapel at some point during the day. They could go in the morning at eight, midday at twelve-thirty, or in the evening at seven. On Wednesdays they usually went in the morning because they helped out with the children's program on Wednesday nights at church, but on Fridays they went in the evening, and it was always a nice end to their week together.

By that Friday Seth was having some serious concerns about Kerri, and he decided to share them with Amber after Chapel. They had already decided they were going to hang out here tonight rather than going into town to see a movie or something. They had been spending a lot of their time together on the weekends with their other friends, either on campus or off, but tonight he had requested time alone with her.

They went for a walk and enjoyed the peacefulness of the campus. Seth loved being here, and he had made a lot of new friends as well as having all those he came here with, but he still preferred time alone with Amber to any of his other relationships. He was looking forward to next year when they would have their own private apartment to share and have that guaranteed time alone no matter how busy their schedules were.

He told her that by the lake and kissed her affectionately, something he had been keeping to a minimum during the last six weeks, but tonight he needed it. She'd always had an ability to excite him physically while relaxing him emotionally, and he didn't realize how much he needed that until he was completely caught up in the tender moment. Some of his anxiety about the future had been creeping in lately, especially with midterms coming up next week. He wanted to do well but had serious studying to do for a couple of his classes.

"I think we should get married in May," he said.

She laughed. They had been discussing possible wedding dates earlier today when they had lunch together, but they hadn't decided if they were going to get married at the beginning, middle, or end of the summer. They were considering going back to camp and getting married the last weekend before they would return here, but he didn't know if he wanted to wait that long or spend another summer seeing her every day but having to keep his distance.

"May sounds nice," she said.

"Really?"

"Yes."

He kissed her again and let it rest for now, but he was somewhat serious, and he knew she was too. They had decided to make a definite decision by the first of the year, which was still three months away, but he liked the thought of getting married at the beginning of the summer rather than the end of it.

"Are you okay?" she asked him once they were walking again. He was thinking more about them, and he was content in their relationship, but he knew she sensed his anxiety about other things.

"I'm worried about Kerri," he said. "Does she seem okay to you?"

"She seems thoughtful," Amber said. "More quiet than usual, but I thought maybe that's because I'm not used to seeing her so much."

"I know she's trying to sort out her future, and I'm not really worried about her, just wishing I knew how to help more."

"I don't think you can. This is something she's going to have to figure out for herself. When she talks, I hear her saying a lot of the things I went through last year before I knew if we were going to the same school or not. Her concerns are different than mine, but I think it comes from the same place."

"Where?"

"The unknown. Feeling like she has to have everything figured out when there's no clear path."

"You mean like us trying to figure out when we're getting married and what to do with next summer?"

"Yeah, like that." She laughed. "And if I should take one less class next semester so I can have more time to write, and if I should go for a definite major or just take classes that interest me."

"I haven't heard you mention any of that."

"I know. I've learned to keep those questions mostly between God and me. I think Kerri is looking for answers she's not supposed to know yet, and I feel that way too, but I'm expecting God to show me at the right time."

Chapter Thirteen

On Saturday morning Kerri did what she had been doing every Saturday for the last month, catching a ride into town with Adam and Lauren, who always worked all day together at Tony's. They would drop her off at the bicycle rental store where she would rent a bike for the day and spend several hours exploring the city.

She loved California. The weather had been really nice so far. She knew rainy weather was coming, but she wanted to enjoy this while it lasted, and she loved the small town that was only fifteen minutes from the campus. From the open plaza and wonderful shops, to the community redwood park where she could ride her bike and enjoy the solitude of a safe setting. The first Saturday she had done this with a group of others, but since then she'd come alone. It gave her time to think.

She spent the morning riding along the bay, grabbed lunch at a deli, and rode to the park to walk to one of her favorite places among the towering redwoods. She liked to write in her journal here, and she was anxious to get started with the second devotional book in a series she had bought yesterday.

She had picked up the first one a month ago at the campus bookstore, and she had devoured it in a month. Every lesson had spoken so deeply to her heart she couldn't go a day without doing the next one.

Her relationship with God was going through the roof right now. God had a lot to show her, and yet with each new thing she learned, she only wanted more. She was unsettled about her future and at peace with it at the same time. She believed God would lead her, but she wanted to know where, and every day she woke up with the thought: 'Today might be the day He fills in that missing piece,' so she was anxiously looking for it and trying to wait patiently too.

The question at the end of the first lesson in the new devotional book described perfectly how she felt:

Do you currently feel you need some light from heaven to shine on you? What do you feel you need most from God?

She took a moment to collect her thoughts and then began writing and didn't stop for several minutes. Her words were random—everything from wanting to know how God was leading her career-wise, to various relationship needs she had, to wanting to grow closer to God and have a deep and intimate connection to Him. She concluded her prayer by quoting some favorite verses from The Psalms she had come across recently:

*Show me your ways, O LORD, teach me your paths;
guide me in your truth and teach me, for you are God
my Savior, and my hope is in you all day long.*

She went to her favorite coffee place when she was finished and did her studying there, browsed the surrounding shops, picked up a gift for her sister whose birthday was coming up in a couple of weeks, and then returned her bike and walked the distance to Tony's for her usual late-afternoon "job". It had become a habit for her to help Kevin with making pizza from four o'clock to five, or whenever it got busy and he kicked her out because she was too slow to work during the dinner rush.

"Hi, Kerri," he said when she arrived in the kitchen, coming over to give her a hug like always. "You're late today."

"It's only 4:05," she defended.

"You're late," he repeated.

"Sorry. I have midterms coming up."

"All right," he said as if that was an acceptable excuse.

She put on an apron and turned to wash her hands at the sink. "What would you do if I didn't show up one of these Saturdays? Fire me?"

"My dad fires people."

She laughed. "But he didn't hire me, you did."

"He's the one who said you could work here."

"But you're the one who keeps asking me to come back."

He got a confused look on his face. "You don't want to work here?"

She laughed and dried her hands on a paper towel. "Of course I do. I'm teasing you."

He didn't laugh or respond in any way. She was trying to get more into his world, but humor was a difficult area. A lot of people here knew how to laugh and joke with him in the right way, but she hadn't figured it out yet.

An order came up as she stepped over to the pizza-making counter, and he let her make most of it without interrupting her work. She had been slowly learning all the details of making the perfect pizza in Kevin's book, and she was often amazed at the things he pointed out, especially the amount of each topping. She had memorized some of the simple things like how many pepperoni slices went on each size of pizza they made, although she often had to rearrange them to make them fit perfectly. Today it was something he had never been so exact about.

"There are only nine onion rings," he said. "There should be one more."

"I like it with nine," she said to see how he would react.

"It should be ten," he restated.

She took another one from the bin. "Where?"

"Right there," he said, pointing to a spot that didn't seem any more prominent to her than another.

She obeyed and then turned to him and said, "How about eleven this time?"

He caught on that she was teasing him. "No, just ten. You're silly, Kerri."

She laughed. "If I was running this place, I'd put eleven."

"You don't run this place. My dad does."

She smiled, finished the pizza off with a light layer of cheese and said, "Actually, I think you do. Is this what you want to do for the rest of your life?"

She was asking him seriously, but she was surprised at his equally serious response. "No. That's why I'm going to school."

"What do you want to do when you finish?"

"I'm not sure."

She smiled. It was always good for her to hear she wasn't the only one without a definite career goal. "You would be a good teacher," she said. "You taught me how to make the perfect pizza."

He looked at her, and she knew he didn't think he was done teaching her that. She laughed and tried to tickle him, but his reflexes were too quick, and he grabbed her hands.

"No playing in the kitchen," he warned in his serious tone.

"Or what? You'll fire me?"

He stared at her curiously for a moment. When she had said that earlier, he'd taken it seriously, but this time he seemed to recollect her teasing tone. "Do you want to get fired?"

She smiled and answered seriously. "No. This is the best job I've ever had."

Tony came up behind them and stuck an order on the first clip. "I think we need to start paying you," he said, "and talk you into coming in more often. I'm going to need a new pizza maker next year. What do you think, Kev? Could she handle this job?"

Kevin appeared skeptical. "Seth would be better. He's faster."

"Seth can't work full-time and neither can she, so maybe we'll train them both. What do you think, Kerri? Are you interested?"

"Yeah, maybe," she said. Coming here every Saturday had become one of her favorite times of the week, but she wasn't sure it would be the same without Kevin. "I'll think about it."

"Did Kev tell you about his recital next Saturday?"

"No," she said, turning back to Kevin who had begun to work on the new order. "What recital?"

"Piano," he said. "It's the mid-term performance."

"Can I come?" she asked.

"Yes. Anybody can come." He told her where and when, and she asked if she needed to buy a ticket. "No. It's free."

"I'll be there," she said. "Who's going to make pizza while you're gone?"

"I don't know. My dad figures that out."

"Well, it can't be me because I'm going to be there too."

He shook his head. "It can't be you because—"

"Oh, hush!" she said, laughing and nudging him out of the way so she could work on the new pizza. "I'm much better than I was a month ago."

She reached for the shredded mozzarella to put on top of the sauce, but Kevin stopped her from sprinkling it on.

"Uh, Kerri?"

"What?" she asked, wondering what it was this time. Did he want her to start counting the cheese shreds too?

"This one is *no cheese*," he said, pointing to the slip.

She felt embarrassed. "No cheese? Who orders a pizza with no cheese?"

"Um, Larry," he said, looking at the name on the slip.

She let the cheese fall back into the bin and laughed. "Why do you put up with me?"

"I don't know," he said. "I just do."

She read the slip more carefully and began putting on the correct toppings. When she was almost finished, she said what she was thinking. "I'm glad you do, because this is one of the highlights of my week."

"Are you sure you want to go to my recital? My dad would probably let you work all through dinner."

She smiled. Kevin called for Adam to come get the pizza she had finished, and once they were alone again she responded.

"I didn't mean making pizza," she said. "I meant spending an hour with you. That's the highlight of my week."

He smiled, and she thought she detected more of a genuine emotional response from him. He didn't say anything, but he appeared to be thinking about something. She waited to see if she was right.

"We always go out to dinner after my recitals," he finally said. "D-Do you want to come?"

"We?"

"My mom, dad, sister, and me."

It was the first time he had ever talked to her on a purely personal level rather than about making pizza or answering her questions. "Sure, I'd love to," she said.

He didn't say anything else, and when another order was placed in front of them, they both went to work. The party had ordered three pizzas, and it was one order after another from then on. She always stayed until they began to get behind and Kevin politely but adamantly dismissed her and would call Blake over to help him instead.

But tonight she kept working, and he didn't kick her out, so she didn't leave. And she wasn't certain, but he didn't seem to be as picky about her work as he usually was. In fact, he seemed distracted, and he messed up on one of the pizzas. He had to toss it and start over, and she had never seen him do that before.

Tony finally commented on her continued presence at six-thirty. "I see he didn't kick you out tonight."

"No, not yet," she said, glancing at Kevin and giving him a wide smile. "I must be doing something right."

"Blake's here," Kevin said. "You can go if you want."

"I'm fine," she said. "I'll stay if you don't mind."

"I don't mind."

His monotone voice and detached demeanor had returned. After his dad stepped away, they finished the new orders and then had a bit of a break. She turned to him and said what she was thinking, wanting that personal connection with him she had managed to find earlier.

"Thanks for letting me stay. Can I do this every Saturday?"

"Next week is my recital," he said.

"I mean after that."

"After that we're going out to dinner."

She laughed.

"What's so funny?"

"Nothing," she said, deciding she would wait and mention it again the next time she was here. "You're right. I'm busy next Saturday."

She worked until seven when Adam and Lauren were finished with their shift. Normally she waited for them in the dining area and did some studying while eating a personal pizza she made for herself, but tonight she hadn't had a chance to eat, so she ate with them and Kevin, who took his dinner break then too. She knew she was going to be up late tonight and would have more studying to do tomorrow, but it was worth it. She really liked spending time with Kevin. He wasn't like anyone she had ever met.

He was so simple at times, and so complex too. She was trying to figure him out and yet not caring if she did or didn't—except for that brief moment earlier when she had broken through somehow and then lost it, and she didn't know how to get it back. She wanted it back.

Kevin told them 'good night' and went back to the kitchen before the rest of them finished eating. But before they left, Kerri went to the kitchen to ask him something. He was working diligently on a pizza, but he was alone, so she went over and asked him for a hug. She usually got one before she left the kitchen, but he had walked out with her earlier.

He stopped what he was doing, wiped his hands on the towel on his shoulder, and turned to give her the requested hug.

"What should I wear to your recital?" she asked.

He stepped back and shrugged. "I don't know."

"What will you be wearing?"

"My black suit."

"With a bow tie or a straight one?"

"A bow tie."

She smiled. "Okay. Will you wear that to dinner too?"

"Not the tie and jacket," he said. "I get too hot."

"Okay. I'll see you there next Saturday. Thanks for inviting me. I'm so excited about hearing you play."

He smiled. "Yeah. I'm pretty good."

She smiled again and kissed him on the cheek. "I'm sure you are. I can't wait."

Chapter Fourteen

By Wednesday afternoon Kerri only had one mid-term to go, and she thought she had done fine with the others. She needed to study for her Old Testament exam tomorrow, but once she finished up at The Oasis in another hour, she would have all evening.

It was slow at the moment, so she made herself a peach smoothie and sat behind the counter with six weeks of notes in front of her, getting in a good ten minutes of studying before someone approached the counter. Looking up, she saw the familiar face and smiled.

"Hi, Josiah," she said, setting her notebook aside and hopping off the stool. "What can I get for you today? The usual?"

"I just finished my last mid-term, so I think I'll splurge today. Give me two cookies instead of only one, and I'll take chocolate milk instead of regular."

She laughed. Josiah was one of those guys who wasn't afraid to still be a kid instead of acting all cool and mature, and yet in her opinion he was more mature than a lot of the freshman guys here. He was up there in the league with her brother. She didn't see him all that often—mostly when she was working here—but she had decided she really liked him.

Handing him the two cookies on a small plate along with his carton of chocolate milk, she took his money in exchange and asked him what he was going to do now that his midterms were over.

"Start studying for the next ones, I guess. My Western Civ prof gave us a gazillion pages to read by Monday."

"Oh, joy," she said. "I think I'm going to try and avoid that class. Seth says it's the worst."

"Yeah, pretty much. What are you taking instead?"

"Psychology."

"Do you like it?"

"Yeah, it's interesting. I'm thinking I might want to do something in that realm of life, but I'm still figuring that out."

"Take your time," he said. "No use trying to figure out what God isn't ready to show you yet."

"But you know."

"But I didn't until a month ago."

"Oh? And why is that?"

Some other people came in and approached the counter. "It's kind of a long story," he said. "Maybe some other time."

"Okay," she said. "Enjoy your milk and cookies."

He turned away with a smile, and she served the next person in line. It stayed busier after that until she was off at six, and then she left to go spend her evening studying in the room. It was always nice and quiet on Wednesdays because Amber and Seth worked with the children's program at church, Lauren and Adam worked at Tony's, and Chad and Jessica usually went to Chapel at seven and then spent the rest of the evening downstairs studying together.

The names of Old Testament people and places were starting to run together when the phone rang at seven-thirty, and she welcomed the break. She expected it to be her mom because she knew this was one of the best times to catch her, but it wasn't. It was Josiah.

"Hi, Josiah," she replied to his shy introduction.

"Hi," he said. "How's the studying going?"

"A little mind-numbing at the moment. How's the reading?"

"About the same." He laughed. "We're only halfway through our first semester of college. I don't think this is a good sign."

"I know. These classes are tough! Can we go back to high school now?"

"Exactly," he said. "Wouldn't that be nice? I didn't appreciate it enough when I was there."

"Me neither."

There was a slight pause, and then Josiah spoke again. "Anyway, the reason I'm calling is because I keep thinking about what I told you earlier about my long story, and I'm wondering if you might like to actually hear it sometime? I've talked to Seth about it, but I feel like I could use a girl's perspective."

"Is it about a girl?"

"Yes and no. It's more about my friend and his girlfriend, but I'm concerned for both of them, and I'm not sure what to do."

"Okay," she said. "When would be a good time for you?"

"Saturday?"

"I can't Saturday," she said not wanting to give up her solo time during the day, and she was going to Kevin's piano recital in the evening. "How about Sunday?"

"Sure, that works for me."

"Would you like to have lunch?"

"Sure. Here or in town?"

"Here is fine. I have to be at church at four-thirty for my girls' disciple group, but I'm free until then."

"Okay. Thanks, Kerri. And just so you know, I'm interested in getting to know you better too. Is that still okay?"

She smiled. "Yes, I'd like that."

"Okay, I'll let you get back to your studying now."

"Will I see you on Friday?"

"Yes, I'll stop by," he said shyly, and she laughed. He had been coming to The Oasis regularly whenever she was working.

"You're not usually there on Sundays," she commented, suddenly realizing that.

"I go to the worship gathering they have on Sunday evenings."

"I've heard it's good," she said. "I might get my hours changed so I can go. You must like it."

"Yes. It's different. A lot of music, and the pastor is a good speaker. He makes me think about God differently. More real, I guess. More in touch with our generation."

She had a thought, and she went with it. "I think I will see if there's another night I can work instead of Sunday. I have to rush to get back here by six."

"I'd love to see you there," he said. "I think you'd like it."

"Oh? Are you an expert on me?"

"Definitely not. Seth tells me good luck with that."

She laughed. "You've been talking to Seth about me?"

"He talks very highly of you, and I've been listening."

"Don't be afraid to form your own opinions. I can't even figure myself out, especially lately."

"We'll have a lot to talk about then."

"I guess we will."

"Okay, Kerri. Have a good night."

"You too, Josiah. Enough reading. Go play a video game or something."

"I think I'll do that. See you Friday."

"Okay. Bye."

Kerri hung up the phone, and she had a good feeling in her heart. When she had first met Josiah six weeks ago, he seemed quiet and shy, but it just took him a few weeks to get comfortable around new people. She had heard enough from Seth and seen enough for herself to know he was a really nice guy, and she was looking forward to spending time with him, and curious about the story he had to tell.

She enjoyed the moment of wondering if he could be the one she had spent the last two years praying and waiting for, but she didn't dwell on it too long. Only time would tell on that, and she had more studying to do right now. When Amber arrived at nine, her mind was mostly mush again, but they quizzed each other a bit, and she felt like she would probably do all right.

"Guess what?" she said before Amber got up from her bed. Jessica and Lauren weren't back yet.

"What?"

"Josiah asked me out."

"He did?"

"Yes. We're having lunch on Sunday."

"That's great! I'm so excited for you. He is really nice."

"I know. I'm excited too. He wants to tell me about everything that happened with his friend and how he ended up here. Do you know anything about that?"

"A little," she said. "But I think I'll let him tell you. I just heard some from Seth, and I wouldn't want to tell you anything wrong."

Lauren came in, and Amber got up to get ready for bed. Lauren followed her but then came back after she was in her pajamas. Kerri wanted to tell her about Josiah too, but Lauren spoke first.

"I heard you're going to Kevin's piano recital on Saturday."

"Yeah. I forgot to tell you that. I can't wait to hear him play."

"He's excited about you being there," she said. "He was telling everybody in the kitchen tonight."

"He was?"

"Yes," she laughed. "And some of the people who don't have to work on Saturday asked him if they could come too, and he was like, 'No, just Kerri.'"

"Why? He told me anyone can come."

"Who knows? It's Kevin. I think it's neat you're going. He doesn't let a lot of people into his world, you know? You're a good one to be there."

"What makes you say that? I feel like I never know what I'm doing or if I'm saying the right thing."

"You must be doing something right because he's excited about it. Did you know you're supposed to dress up? It's a pretty formal thing."

"Yeah, I figured. I'm looking forward to it. Did you know I'm going out to dinner with them too?"

Lauren got a confused look on her face. "You are? With his family?"

"Yes. He asked me."

Lauren stared at her. "Oh, my gosh! Kerri! Do you know how huge that is?"

"What?"

"Going out to dinner with his family? Not even Blake has done that."

"Why not?"

"In Kevin's mind, dinner with his family after a recital is the most sacred, always-the-same thing. They go to the same restaurant. They sit in the same places at the same table. They stay until a certain time. Last spring when our whole family went to the recital with Blake, he refused to go to dinner because Jenna invited her boyfriend. He went to the pizza place and played pinball for three hours instead."

"Jenna? Is that his sister?"

"Yes. And Blake told me one time Tony closed the pizza place because he couldn't get enough people to work, but he wasn't going to miss Kevin's recital and the dinner. Something like that would set him back for weeks."

"Set him back?"

"He can get really closed-off sometimes. Something will trigger something in his mind—something isn't right—and he can't function until he can get it all straight in his head again."

"Do you think I shouldn't go?"

"No! Not if he invited you. If you back out, that would be disastrous!"

Kerri felt strange and perplexed, but very privileged. "Why do you think he asked me? I barely know him."

Lauren smiled at her. "Maybe he wants to change that."

Kerri didn't realize she forgot to tell Lauren about Josiah until after she was gone. Deciding to get ready for bed, she tried to put Kevin out of her mind, but when Jessica came upstairs at ten-thirty, she was still lying there awake thinking about it. She hadn't even turned out the light.

"Sorry," Jessica whispered. "I kicked Chad out at ten, but he kept me outside talking for another half-hour. He can really talk when he gets going. Tonight he was talking about how he's becoming more and more convinced God is calling him to be a pastor. Not a youth pastor, but a pastor, pastor. Can you imagine me being a pastor's wife? Get real!"

Kerri laughed.

"Anyway, that's why I'm so late."

"It's fine," she said. "I'm not tired yet, just tired of studying. I'm so ready for this week to be over."

"Tough day? I haven't seen you since this morning."

"Not really tough, just long. And, interesting."

"Oh?" Jessica asked as she began to get undressed. "How so?"

"Josiah asked me out," she said, almost as an afterthought. In light of what Lauren had said about Kevin, it had taken a serious back seat to that.

"He did? Are you excited?"

"Yeah, I am."

"But?"

She decided she didn't want to get into it right now. "But nothing. I'm excited, I just have a lot on my mind."

"Like what?" Jessica asked, taking her pajamas from her drawer and putting them on and then sitting on the edge of her bed like she could talk all night. Kerri decided to share.

"Have you ever had something happen you didn't think was a big deal at the time, but then later you found out it was?"

"Yes. What happened?"

"Honestly, I'm not sure. But I think I'll find out on Saturday. Did I mention I'm ready for this week to be over?"

"What's happening on Saturday? You're going out with Josiah?"

"No, I'm having lunch with him on Sunday. On Saturday I'm—I'm going out with Kevin, I think."

"Kevin who?"

"Kevin—from the pizza place. Tony's son?"

"The guy you make pizza with on Saturdays?"

"Yes."

"He asked you out?"

"No, not really. Well, maybe. He invited me to his piano recital and out to dinner with his family, and I didn't think it was a big deal, but then Lauren just told me otherwise. It's a big deal for Kevin."

Jessica smiled and then laughed. "How is it that the girl I know who is the most selective about whom she dates managed to get asked out by a guy without realizing it?"

Kerri laughed and put her hands over her face. "I have no idea. Jess! What am I going to do?"

"Calm down," she said, laughing again and rising from the bed. "Just have fun and see what happens. If there's one thing I know about you, you always rise to the occasion."

"Calm down? Have fun? Jess!" She sat up on her elbows, but it was too late. Jessica had disappeared into the bathroom. Lying down and letting the enormity of this hit her in full force, the only thing she could do was pray.

God? How did I get myself into this? What have I done? This 'living one day at a time and not worrying about tomorrow' sucks! I can't do that. I have to—I don't know, something! What am I supposed to do? Whatever it is, tell me, and I'll do it.

Be still and know that I am God, Kerri. Relax. Calm down. Rest in Me.

I can't!

Rest, Kerri. It's the only thing you can do. Nothing's broken, so don't try to fix it. You've prayed, and I'm answering. Just rest. Rest in My love. Rest in My grace. I know what I'm doing. Trust Me.

Chapter Fifteen

Adam needed to go to the campus bookstore to get more pencils. He didn't usually use them, and he only had a couple in his room, but he needed better ones for taking his midterms than he had been using thus far. He hadn't been in the bookstore since purchasing his books and a few supplies during the first week, and he didn't notice the girl working the cash register until he was almost at the front of the line.

He would have stepped away and gone to the other, but it was closed currently. Placing the pencils on the counter, he thought Abby might not recognize him, but she did, and an immediate smile came to her face as if they had been the best of friends.

"Well, I finally run into you," she said. "How are you, Adam?"

"Fine. How are you?"

"Great! Don't you just love it here? It reminds me of camp."

"Yeah, it's kind of like that. I even still work in the kitchen."

She laughed at his little joke, and he heard the alarms going off in his head to end this conversation as soon as possible and get out of here. Abby had a very friendly appeal that was difficult to resist without being completely rude. And since he wanted to leave the past in the past, he didn't want to let her know how deeply all of that had affected him. He may not have touched her and made out with her like she had wanted him to, but his mind sometimes headed down that road.

He didn't wait for her to put the pencils into a bag, and he paid with exact change, stepping away with a quick 'See you,' as if he was in a hurry, but her voice called after him.

"Come by my room sometime, and we'll catch up," she said, tacking on her dorm hall and room number.

He acknowledged her visually but not verbally and headed out the door. He had absolutely no intention of ever going to her dorm room, and yet that night he dreamed about her. He woke up in a cold sweat, and he felt ashamed for dreaming about her in that way. He knew it was just a dream and not his true desire, and yet it left him with an unsettled and guilty feeling all day. He didn't see Lauren until two-thirty when they met to have a little time together before his next class, and he couldn't look her in the eye.

It was a dream. You didn't do anything. Stop feeling guilty.

If Lauren noticed his altered behavior, she didn't say anything, and when he kissed her before they parted, he made it a good one.

She smiled. He didn't usually kiss her like that in the middle of the day.

On the way to Chambers Hall, he knew he should have said he saw Abby yesterday, but he didn't know if he could do so without letting her know how deeply it had affected him. He knew he hadn't done anything wrong, but he knew it could be hurtful to her to know his thoughts had been on someone else.

The following day was Friday, and his mind wasn't on it so much. When he saw Lauren at lunch, he felt back to his normal self, and the thought of Abby and having the dream about her only came to mind a few random times. He didn't dwell on it, and by the time he headed for his dorm room that afternoon, he was looking forward to an evening with Lauren and wasn't thinking about it at all.

He met her for dinner, and they remained in the cafeteria after they were finished eating, talking and catching up on their week. Lauren was feeling stressed about school because she wasn't sure what she wanted to study, wasn't enjoying any of her classes, and she wasn't sure she had done too well on her exams this week. He tried to encourage her, and she seemed a little better by the time they left to go into town to see a movie, but he tried to treat her extra special and be romantic during their time together, especially when there was a sweet love scene in the movie, and he gave her a kiss matching the one the two characters shared.

She was pretty snuggly after that, and when a more serious love scene took place where it was obvious the couple ended up having sex, even though they didn't show it directly on screen, he allowed his mind to wander to having a time like that with Lauren someday. After they were married, of course, but his thoughts were vivid.

After the movie they drove back to the campus and sat in his truck to finish the conversation they were having, and then he started kissing her. She felt really good to him tonight, and she seemed to need his affection more than usual. When his hands started roaming and slipped underneath her shirt to touch her bare skin, he heard alarms going off in his head that this was going too far, but he ignored them.

She felt too good to him, and he justified his affection, knowing they could only go so far in his truck. They weren't even in a secluded part of the parking lot. Someone could walk by at any time. He was all right.

"I'm not comfortable with that, Adam," he heard Lauren say, but it didn't fully register until she said his name a little more adamantly.

"Adam!"

He snapped out of where his mind had been going, which was ahead of his hands, but he suddenly realized his hands had made it farther than he realized.

"I'm sorry," he said, feeling strange. How could he not have known that?

She forgave him easily, but when he placed his hands in a more appropriate place and tried to kiss her again, a picture of his dream with Abby flashed into his mind, and he pulled away abruptly.

"Are you okay?" she asked.

He felt ashamed for his thoughts, and he felt out of control of his desires. "I think I need to get out of here," he said.

She didn't protest, and they got out of the truck. He walked with her toward her dorm, and he apologized again.

"It's okay," she said, but he knew it wasn't. He had promised her better. What was the matter with him?

It was already after ten, so he told her good-night instead of keeping her out later. She was fine with that, and after a brief kiss, he went to his dorm and upstairs to his room. Seth was there, but not Chad or Josiah, so he decided to talk to him. He just told him everything, something he had wanted to do with Lauren, but he couldn't. It seemed too hurtful to say to her, but Seth was a guy, so he knew he would understand better.

He felt like a jerk, but Seth was easy on him. He asked if he wanted to be in this relationship with Lauren or if he was beginning to feel it wasn't right, but he had no such feelings.

"I've loved her from the moment I first kissed her, and nothing has changed. Why would I be thinking of someone else in my dreams or when I'm kissing Lauren? I could choose to think about Abby if I wanted to, but I don't."

"I'm not sure why, Adam, but stuff like that buries itself deep in our natural minds as guys, and it takes supernatural power to get rid of it. First you need to pray. Ask God to remove it, and if that is truly your heart's desire, I believe He will. Second, you need to tell Lauren. Don't try and handle it yourself, let her help you in your weakness and ask her to pray for you.

"And third, you need to treat your relationship with her as sacred. Nothing messes with it that shouldn't be there. If that means you can't be alone with her, then don't be. If that means you need to be more selective about the movies you watch to keep both of you from seeing others getting involved in premarital sex, then you do that. If you need to get your relationship with God more right so you can be the man Lauren needs you to be, do that. Don't let things slide, even a little bit. Love is sacred. Treat it that way."

***

When Lauren came into the room and began to get ready for bed, Amber could see that something was wrong. Lauren always had a happy and carefree spirit, especially after she spent time with Adam, but it was absent tonight, and Amber got an uneasy feeling.

She hesitated to say anything because she still didn't know Lauren all that well. If something was wrong, she thought Lauren might go talk to Kerri, but when she didn't, Amber went ahead and said something.

"Are you okay, Lauren?"

Lauren sat on the edge of her bed in her pajamas, but she didn't pull back the blankets and crash like she usually did. She sat there quietly for a moment, and when she didn't say anything else, Amber laid her laptop aside and went to sit beside her.

"What happened?"

Lauren started crying, and Amber held her. She didn't say anything, so Amber asked if she wanted her to get Kerri.

"No," she said. "I'm all right."

"Is this about Adam?"

"Yes."

She waited for her to continue.

"He did something I didn't like when we were kissing tonight. He's never done that before. He stopped, but I—It wasn't that big of a deal—" her voice trailed off.

"I'm sorry, Lauren," Amber said, meaning that with all of her heart. If Lauren was talking about some jerk she had been out with a couple of times, she would tell her she deserved better and to forget about him, but she wasn't. She was talking about Adam. One of the good ones. Someone like Seth.

"I never thought he would do something like that," she said. "I'm afraid next time—I don't want to get into that kind of battle."

Amber knew what she meant. "I don't want to sound trite, Lauren, but pray for him. Ask God to deal with whatever's going on in his heart and mind that made him do that."

"And if it keeps happening?"

"I could have Seth talk to him for you, but you might need to stop seeing him."

"I don't want to lose him, Amber. I love him."

"I know you do. Love him enough to walk away and give him time and space to work through it, if it comes to that. If you love him, you won't let him do things he shouldn't, because the reality is it doesn't just hurt you, Lauren, it hurts him too."

Chapter Sixteen

On Friday morning Blake woke up feeling very excited. Colleen was coming to visit him this weekend and would be arriving this evening. He was going to pick her up at the airport, and he couldn't wait to see her. He had gone to visit her last month in Portland. That weekend had gone by way too fast. He knew this one probably wouldn't go much slower, but he wanted to see her, even if it was for a short time.

He called her every night. Whether he was at Tony's, the church, or his dorm, he couldn't help it. Even if he didn't have anything to say, he liked hearing her voice. Seeing her tonight and getting to kiss her sweet lips would be even better. He had a day to get through first, including one more mid-term. He was glad his professor had delayed it until Friday because he had needed more time to study, but he was also ready for this long week to be over. Heading downstairs to get breakfast before his first class, he met Lauren like usual on Fridays. She had already gotten her food and was waiting for him at a table by the window. It was their standing date that gave Adam one morning he could sleep in. His first class on

Friday wasn't until one o'clock, and he also didn't have to work in the kitchen.

"Did you hear about Kevin asking Kerri to go to his recital tomorrow?" she asked as soon as he sat down.

"Yes, Kevin told me. Several times."

"Did you know he asked her to go to dinner with them too?"

Blake stared at his sister. "He did? With his family?"

"Yes."

"No, I didn't hear that. Kevin didn't say anything about it."

"I know, me neither. Do you think his family knows?"

He shrugged. "Tony didn't say anything, but maybe he assumed I already knew."

"I'm a little worried for Kerri."

He took a drink of milk before responding. "Why?"

"She doesn't know what Kevin can be like. What if he forgot he asked her and when she tries to go, he freaks out?"

"I don't think he would forget. Kevin doesn't forget anything."

"What if he decides he doesn't want her to go?"

"He wouldn't ask her if he didn't want her to go."

"Are you going to be seeing him before tomorrow night?"

"Wasn't planning on it," he said, taking a bite of his eggs. "I have this weekend off, remember?"

"I know, but maybe you could drop by tonight before you pick up Colleen."

He laughed. "I think I'd rather wait and see what happens."

"Blake! This is serious."

"All right, I'll call Tony later. Calm down, Lauren. Kerri's a big girl. If anyone can handle this, she can."

Blake understood what Lauren was saying, but at the same time, he had seen enough of Kevin with Kerri to know they seemed to know how to deal with each other. He had never once had to step in and help Kerri out of a sticky situation, and he had never seen Kevin be more patient with someone than Kerri.

He ended up forgetting about calling Tony until he was on the way to get Colleen from the airport. He didn't have time to stop, so he decided to pick up Colleen first and then take her to the pizza place. He wanted to do that anyway to introduce her to all of his friends.

When he saw her inside the small terminal, an instant smile came to his face, and when she saw him, she returned it.

"Hey, beautiful," he said, taking her into his arms and holding her close for several moments. "How did you like that little plane from San Francisco?"

She laughed. "It wasn't so bad. Definitely worth it."

After a few brief kisses, he led her out to the car. They talked casually along the way, and he felt a usual carefree feeling with her at his side. He put her bag in the back and turned to give her another kiss, but she spoke first.

"Guess what?"

"What?"

"I'm transferring to Lifegate next semester."

He laughed. "What?"

"I'm doing it, Blake. I think God wanted me to remain in Portland for a few months to convince me what we have is real and exactly what I want, but He's not going to make me wait to be with you. Even if they don't approve my transfer, I'm coming anyway. I'll work or do whatever I have to do to be here with you."

He closed his eyes and pulled her close to him. "I said I'd move up there, baby."

"You don't belong up there. You belong here, and I belong here with you. No arguing."

He smiled. "I love you."

"I love you too, Blake. Let's have a great weekend together, okay? I need it."

"Me too," he said, kissing her tenderly and with more longing than he had allowed himself to feel before. He had needed to guard his heart a little, just in case she changed her mind about this, or it was another three years before they could be together as much as he wanted.

He took her to the beach on the way back to town, and they didn't arrive at Tony's until almost eight, but when they did, he proudly introduced her to everyone who was working at the time. Kevin was more into meeting her than he thought he would be. He tended to be neutral when he met new people, but he gave Colleen a hug and said, "He talks about you all the time. Colleen, Colleen, Colleen. That's all I ever hear anymore."

"And can you blame me, Kev? Isn't she beautiful?"

"Yes. Like Kerri."

Blake laughed. He'd never heard Kevin comment on a girl's appearance before.

"Why are you laughing?" Kevin asked. "Kerri is beautiful."

"I know. Nothing, Kev. As you were. We're going to go sit down. Make us a good pizza, will you?"

"Sure," he said, going back to his work.

"What was that about?" Colleen asked. "Was he talking about Kerri, Kerri?"

"Yes."

"Does she work here too? I thought only Seth did."

"She helps out sometimes, and I think Kevin has a little crush on her. It is so not like him to say something like that."

Stepping around to the front counter to place their order, he asked Tony the question he was curious to know the answer to himself.

"Do you know that Kevin invited Kerri to dinner tomorrow?"

"Yes."

"Did he do that all on his own, or did you have a hand in it?"

"I mentioned the recital to Kerri, but dinner was completely Kev's idea. I didn't even know about it until yesterday when he reminded me to make the reservations, and he told me I needed to make it for five this time."

"I guess he knows exactly what he's doing then, doesn't he?"

"I think so. And I've prayed for it, but I've never honestly known if I would ever see it."

***

Kerri decided not to say anything to anyone else about going to dinner with Kevin and his family being a big deal. She told Seth about it casually when she saw him at The Oasis on Friday night because she needed to have the car, and he seemed curious but not surprised. He knew they had been getting to know each other. She panicked a little when Seth said maybe he and Amber would come too, but she covered by saying, "I think he likes to invite people, not just have them show up. I might be wrong though. You could ask him."

"Maybe we'll catch the next one," he said. "Colleen's coming tonight, so I'm sure Amber wants to have some time with her. Tell him I want to know when the next one is."

"Okay, I'll tell him," she said.

Josiah arrived at his usual time a few minutes later. He didn't act any differently with her than normal and left her to do her job until later when there was no line, and then he came back to talk to her. She was glad to see him being himself instead of acting weird around her because he'd asked her out.

Colleen spent the night in their room, and they all learned she had decided to transfer here next semester. Kerri couldn't blame her. Guys like Blake didn't come along every day. She wondered if she had foolishly let him get away from her this summer. She had known he liked her, even though he never said so directly. He seemed too serious for her so she had resisted it, and he had eventually turned his eyes elsewhere. She knew it was just as well. He and

Colleen were so happy, but she was definitely looking for a guy like him.

On Saturday morning she decided not to go into town with Lauren and Adam. Seth had said she could have the car today, and she didn't feel like going for a bike-ride. At noon she heard the redwood park calling her name, and she picked up a sandwich from the dining hall and drove into town to spend an hour or two walking the trails and sitting in her usual place to write in her journal and do the next lesson in her devotional book. She was deep in thought at the picnic table when she heard someone say her name. She turned and saw Kevin standing there.

"Hey, what are you doing here?" she asked, smiling at him.

"Going for a walk," he said.

"Are you nervous about tonight?"

"Yes."

"Can you sit for awhile?"

"Sure," he said, sitting down right beside her instead of on the opposite side of the table. She didn't mind, but she had to turn her body to face him. Her Bible pages were flapping in the mild breeze, so she closed them.

"I'm sure you're going to do great," she said. "You always do, right?"

"Yes," he said. "But I still get nervous."

"What helps you relax?"

"Walking. Trees. Sunshine."

"You picked the right place. I love it here."

"Me too."

"Do you come here a lot?"

"Yes."

"Alone?"

"Yes, or with Jenna."

"I'm looking forward to meeting her tonight. Does she know I'm coming?"

"Yes."

That made her feel better. "I'm glad you invited me to dinner too," she said, just to make sure he hadn't forgotten or she had misunderstood.

"I'm glad you're coming," he said.

"Will you meet me in the concert hall afterwards, or should I meet you at the restaurant?"

"I'll meet you," he said. "You won't know where to go."

"That's true," she said. "But you could give me directions."

He laughed.

"What? You don't think I can follow directions?"

"No, not to there."

She laughed and didn't argue with him. She had gotten lost before when she had driven somewhere she hadn't been familiar with. She had almost missed the turn for the park today because she was used to riding a bike here instead of driving, and it came up more quickly than she was anticipating.

"I think you're beautiful, Kerri."

That came out of nowhere. She wasn't sure what to say. "Thank you."

"I like your laugh and your smile."

"I like yours," she said, taking a really good look at him. He was very cute. Like a little boy in a man's body, physically and emotionally, and yet strangely mature at the same time. "Can I ask you something?"

"Sure."

"What do you believe about God?"

He appeared to not understand the question, but he answered it. "Everything."

"Everything you've been taught?"

"No. Everything that's true."

"What's that?"

He sighed like this could be a long list, but he went ahead and got started. "He made us. He's here, and He's everywhere even though we can't see Him. He's among the stars way out there, and He's in my heart. He loves us. He takes care of us. He lives forever, so we can live forever even after we die. He helps me think and feel and know things. He makes me laugh and smile and makes my heart happy." He paused. "Why? What do you believe?"

"The same," she said. "I was just wondering. You don't talk at work about anything besides work."

"I'm there to work."

"I know you are," she said. "I guess I'll have to meet you someplace else to talk."

"We're talking here."

"Yes, we are. And I like it."

"We can talk tonight at dinner."

"Yes. We'll do that."

"I'm glad you're coming."

"Me too. I heard you don't usually invite anyone."

"No."

"So, why me?"

"Because I want to."

She laughed. "I know, but why? You've known me for a month. You've never invited Blake or Lauren or any of your other friends. Why me, Kevin? What were you thinking when you asked me?"

Ever so gently Kevin slipped his hand around her waist. Leaning his forehead against her temple, he whispered something like he had a secret to tell her.

"I like you, Kerri. When I'm with you, I feel different."

She suddenly realized why she had been feeling so unsettled these last few weeks, and why she enjoyed making pizza with Kevin every Saturday, and why this week had seemed so long compared to the others. Even before she knew this was a big step for Kevin, she had been looking forward to seeing him today. She had been missing him during the week ever since she had first met him.

"You knew I was going to be here today, didn't you?" she said softly.

"Yes."

She always talked his ear off about how she spent her day before going to the pizza place at four. She had talked his ear off about her entire week and a bunch of other stuff she couldn't even remember, but she had a feeling Kevin had remembered every word.

"I like you too, Kevin," she said, looking into his wonderful blue-green eyes and speaking purely from her heart. "When I'm with you, I feel different too."

Chapter Seventeen

Blake couldn't believe how good it felt to have Colleen by his side once again. He knew he had missed her, but the way her presence filled up his heart made him realize just how much. They had spent the morning with Amber, Seth, Chad, and Jessica, and had lunch with them, but then he stole her away for the afternoon to have her all to himself. He needed that deeper connection where they could be completely open and transparent with each other. He didn't have anything specific he wanted to talk to her about, but after ten minutes of walking down the beach, he discovered she did.

"I have something to tell you, and I hope you won't be mad."

"What?" he asked, not feeling too alarmed. She had told him yesterday how much she loved him and wanted to be here with him. Nothing else mattered.

"I spent some time with Chris last weekend."

He knew Chris had bothered her some during the first couple of weeks at school, trying to get her to spend time with him and telling her she should be with him instead. He had backed off eventually, and she hadn't mentioned him since, but Blake knew they saw each other on a regular basis on the small campus.

"How so?" he asked.

"I saw him on Friday at Chapel and he asked if we could talk sometime. He seemed genuinely down, like he really did need to, so I agreed to meet him on Saturday for lunch."

"That doesn't bother me," Blake said. At the end of the summer he had been afraid of losing Colleen, but he'd become more secure with each passing week, and everything Colleen said to him indicated she had no interest in Chris anymore, so he hadn't been worried about it. "What did he want to talk to you about?"

"A lot of stuff," she said. "He's feeling lost right now. He really wanted to go to Vietnam this year, and when that fell through and then he came back and found out he couldn't have me either—It's just a confusing time for him."

Blake could relate. When he had first decided to come to Lifegate, he felt really excited about going to a Christian college and pursuing a life of full-time ministry, but then his first year had been rough and left him wondering if he had been led by God after all. For him the problem had been he was focused more on serving God and doing all this great stuff for Him, rather than being focused on God Himself. Over the summer between his first and second year, he had learned to seek a deeper relationship with Jesus and have everything revolve around that rather than his future plans, and it had made a world of difference.

He had told Colleen that, and he knew Colleen had been caught in the same trap, but she was working her way out of it. She said she had shared that with Chris and it seemed to help, but she got the feeling he didn't understand what she was saying.

"I think it's something you have to experience before you can fully understand it," he said, knowing he had tried to counsel others in the same thing. Some listened and took to heart his advice about going to Jesus with everything, making that time with Him a priority every day, and really listening and going where He led them, but others didn't listen and just kept walking the same confusing and frustrating path, wondering why God seemed so distant.

It was painful to watch, and he was glad Colleen had already heard a lot of it from Amber and had begun taking steps that direction. It was something that had attracted him to her initially because he didn't often hear other girls talking about their relationship with God in real-life, everyday terms. Many Christian girls, and guys, spouted a bunch of clichés and faked a relationship with Him, having absolutely no idea they were doing so.

"I want you to know," Colleen went on, "there was a part of me that thought, 'Maybe I should get back together with Chris so I can help him understand.' I know it's going to take more talking to convince him, and he needs someone who can be asking him, 'Have you been spending time with Jesus? Are you asking Him for direction and waiting for Him to show you? Are you going to Jesus with your struggles, or trying to work them out on your own?' But I wouldn't feel comfortable spending that much time with him if you and I are together. That would be too tempting for

Chris to get caught up in the idea the potential for us to get back together is there."

If Colleen hadn't already told him she was transferring here next semester, he would have felt alarmed, but apparently she had already made her decision on that. "What made you decide not to?"

She stopped walking and turned to face him. "Because I'm in love with you. God is going to have to bring someone else into Chris' life besides me. And I'm sure He will. Chris has a heart for God, I have no doubt about that, he just needs to let God fill him completely instead of trying to find satisfaction in all of his other noble pursuits."

He kissed her and made it last. He couldn't believe the way she made him feel, and he couldn't believe he could make her feel the exact same way. Last night he hadn't been able to kiss her for too long because his desire had been too strong to keep it under control, but today he wanted to show her his affection without needing anything in return.

"What's a beautiful girl like you doing with a guy like me?"

She smiled. "I'm not just beautiful, I'm smart too."

"I can't argue with that," he said.

"I'm glad we're on the same level spiritually. I was thinking about that this week after I talked to Chris. I know you're a lot stronger than me, but I'm getting there. You're what I need, Blake."

"It's not the kissing, huh?"

She laughed. "It's all of it, Blake. All of you. The kissing, and quoting Bible verses at me, and making me laugh, and taking me back to the dorm last night before midnight because you knew you needed to." She paused and added, "I love you. So much."

He kissed her and had a strong desire to take care of Colleen for the rest of his life. She needed him, and he needed her. "I love you too, Colleen. I'm so glad you're going to be here next semester with me."

"And wherever you go from now on," she said. "There's no turning back from here."

***

When Kerri returned to the campus, she didn't have a lot of time before she needed to leave again for Kevin's recital. She hadn't planned to stay at the park so long, but she and Kevin had talked for an hour, and she hadn't wanted to cut him off. She liked listening to him and getting to know him better. He was different away from work and yet the same. More laid-back and talkative, but he didn't usually volunteer information. She had to ask. Her role as a mentor in her youth group and as a peer-counselor at the pregnancy center had prepared her well for getting those to talk who didn't do so easily.

But with Kevin she didn't feel the need to help him understand anything about life or give him advice about what to do. He knew who he was and what he wanted, and he had a very clear picture of right and wrong. Everything was black and white for him. He was open to learning when it was okay to be flexible, but he waited for someone to tell him. He never assumed anything.

Stepping into her dorm room and finding it empty, she had the same thought she'd been having since leaving the park, and while she had been sitting there with Kevin. *Am I his girlfriend now, and is that what I want?* He hadn't said anything of the kind directly, and other than holding her close for a minute when he admitted why he had asked her to come to dinner with his family, he hadn't touched her again except to give her a normal hug beside the car before she left.

She took a shower and remained alone in the room until she was ready to go. When she opened the door to leave, Amber and Seth were about to come inside, and they both commented on her dressy appearance.

"Lauren said it's a formal thing," she said.

"Yeah there's formal, Kerri," Seth said, giving her a hug. "And then there's you. You look really beautiful."

"Thanks," she said. "I need to go. I don't want to be late."

"Okay, bye. Have fun and tell Kevin hi from us."

"I will."

She wasn't sure why she wasn't being more forthright with her brother about this. She was usually open with him about guys she liked or dated, or about any problems she was having, but she supposed that was just it. She didn't know if she liked Kevin as anything more than a friend, if he considered this to be a date, and if she was having a problem or not. She liked Kevin. She wanted to go tonight. She wasn't sure what he was thinking, but she had a certain amount of curiosity to find out, and she honestly didn't know how she would react to anything he said or did.

The school and concert hall were easy to find, and Kevin had said he would meet her outside. He was there with his family, and she had a strange feeling as she approached them, but she tried to act confident and happy to be there. She was happy to be here, but she also had some serious concerns about what his family would think. She knew Tony well, of course, and he'd always been friendly to her and had helped her get into Kevin's world in the first place, but she had never met his mother or his sister. She didn't even know anything about his sister except that her name was Jenna.

Tony was the first to speak to her. "Good evening, Kerri. You look lovely."

"Thank you," she said, seeing she was sufficiently dressed for the occasion. She didn't have any formal dresses here, but she had brought the dress she had worn for graduation, and it was similar to what Jenna was wearing.

Tony went on, introducing her to Kevin's mom and his sister, and they both greeted her warmly. "I've seen you at church," his mother said. "Kevin pointed you out, but he was too shy to introduce us."

"Mom," Kevin said, speaking for the first time. "Don't tell her that."

Kerri turned to him and initiated a hug. "You look handsome," she said for his ears only.

"Thank you. You smell nice."

He needed to go warm up, and she went in with his family to find seats and wait for the performance to begin. She could see by the lengthy program they were going to be here for awhile, and Kevin's name was listed about two-thirds of the way down.

After they were seated, Jenna began asking her questions about herself, and they talked until the opening number. She seemed sweet, and Kerri learned more about her. She was three years older than Kevin, and she taught first grade at a local elementary school. She was also engaged and planning to get married next summer. Kerri wondered if Jenna's fiancé was the same boyfriend Kevin had not allowed to join them for dinner in the past, and she supposed he was. One, because Jenna seemed reluctant to talk about their upcoming wedding plans, and two, because she said they had been dating for almost four years.

***

Kevin felt nervous while he waited backstage for his turn to play. He was glad Kerri was here but felt tense about it at the same time. He wanted to play well for her. He was afraid she wouldn't like it. He knew his pieces were always played technically correct, but he lacked emotion, his teachers and judges always said. He didn't know how to play with emotion.

He saw notes and keys and heard pitch and tones. He could play loud and soft and slow and fast, but exactly how did one play with emotion? He didn't understand the concept. What did emotion have to do with playing the piano?

His dad came to sit with him for a few minutes before his turn came, and his dad's presence helped him to relax, along with his words.

"She's going to love whatever you do, Kev. She's not a piano teacher or a judge; she's your friend, and she's going to love hearing you play. So just play."

"I can't believe she's here. Sh-She's so b-beautiful, Dad. Why is sh-she here?"

"Because you invited her."

His dad left him, and he smiled at the thought. A month ago he never would have imagined inviting anyone to his recital, let alone a beautiful girl he had known for such a short time. He didn't do that. He didn't let people in so quickly. How had she stepped into his world, and why did he like her so much? Why had he felt empty after she left last Saturday? Why had he felt a strong need to see her this afternoon? Why did he feel different when she was near?

"You're up, Kevin," his longtime teacher stepped over to say, interrupting his thoughts about Kerri but not dispelling them completely.

Walking down the hallway and up onto the stage, he could only think about her. And when he sat down to play, his fingers touched the keys and began the memorized piece he had practiced dozens of times, and yet it came out sounding different than he'd ever heard before.

***

Kerri felt nervous for Kevin as he came onto the stage and sat at the grand piano. Thus far all the performances had been good. She had never played the piano or any other instrument, and she was amazed by people who had half the talent of those she'd heard tonight. She knew Kevin had to be of the same caliber, but she had a hard time imagining it. She had noticed he often stuttered when he got tense at work or when he was nervous, like this afternoon when he first approached her and again when she met him outside the concert hall. She wondered if he might have a difficult time playing if his nerves were greater than usual, but as he began to play, that didn't appear to be the case.

She wasn't an expert on piano-playing by any means, but she didn't need to be to know Kevin was quite proficient. She watched him for about a minute and then closed her eyes and just listened. The music took her to another place. A place outside these walls: to the park and its gentle breeze and towering trees; to the ocean and its crashing waves; to making pizza with Kevin in a warm kitchen; to home with her family she had been missing this week; to camp and all the great memories she had there, to sharing the truth with young girls in need of encouragement and guidance and genuine love.

When the music ended, she took a deep breath in the contrasting silence and heard the applause around her begin. She joined in and opened her eyes to see Kevin stand from the piano, take a formal bow, and leave the stage. It wasn't until then she turned to look at his family and saw tears on each of their faces.

Jenna was already looking at her and smiled. "I've never heard him play like that. I don't know what you're doing to my brother, but whatever it is, I hope you don't stop."

Kerri wasn't sure what to think or say, so she remained silent, but the words remained on her mind for the rest of the concert and were echoed by Kevin's parents afterwards when they walked out into the lobby.

"Thanks for coming," his mom said, giving her a hug and sounding choked up. Her next words she could only whisper. "You've reached a part of his heart no one else can."

Tony hugged her also before she could begin to digest those words, and he added his own. "I know you don't know the difference, but that's the way I've always known he could play if someone could figure out how to teach him."

She felt like she needed to escape, and fortunately she needed to use the restroom, so she asked where it was. His mom pointed it out, but she saw Kevin weaving his way through the crowd as she turned to head that direction, so she decided to wait. His family all gave him hugs and told him what a great job he'd done, and Kevin seemed to know he had played differently.

When he turned to face her, he had a really big smile on his face, and he didn't give her a regular hug like she was used to from him. He wrapped his arms around her waist and picked her up off the ground, holding her close to him for a long time.

"You were amazing," she said.

She had been feeling uncomfortable with his family's comments of her invading his heart when she had made absolutely no effort to do so, but being held by Kevin like this—he didn't have to say it. She knew without a doubt in her mind Kevin wanted her in his life in a special way. Somehow she had stepped into his world, and if she hadn't been praying for her future husband for the past two years, she would have run like the wind; but she had been, so she held on tight.

He set her down gently, and for a moment she thought he was going to kiss her, but he simply stroked her cheek and said, "I'm glad you came."

"Me too, Kevin. I really enjoyed it."

Tony interrupted by laying his hand on Kevin's shoulder and giving him gentle instructions. "Kerri needs to use the ladies' room before we go. Remember to have her drive her car back into town. We'll go on ahead to the restaurant, and you can meet us there, all right?"

"All right, Dad."

The three of them turned away and left her and Kevin standing there.

"I'll be right back," she said. "Wait for me?"

"I'll wait outside. It's warm in here."

She felt dazed as she walked to the restroom. When she finished washing her hands at the sink and reapplied her light pink lipstick, she still felt that way.

Before she went back out to meet Kevin, she took a moment to catch her breath and think about what was happening. Tonight was turning out how she had feared after Lauren told her what a big night this was for Kevin, but now that she was in the middle of it, she felt fearless. A little nervous and unsure of what to expect, but not afraid.

Be still and know that I am God.

The familiar words were as clear as she had ever heard them, and they brought her peace.

Okay, Jesus. You brought me here. I don't know where I'm going, but I trust you to lead me. Tonight, and for how many ever tomorrows.

Chapter Eighteen

Seth and Amber had given Blake and Colleen the afternoon to themselves, but they were meeting up with them for dinner along with Chad and Jessica, and Seth was glad to have some time with Blake again. He didn't see him much because they had no classes together, lived in different dorms, worked on different nights at Tony's, and attended different chapel times and church services. About the only time he ever saw him was at church, but it was usually in passing. As a senior this year, Blake's youth intern responsibilities were very great, so he was busy both Sunday mornings and Wednesday nights.

For now he and Amber were attending one worship service on Sunday mornings and then working with the grade school kids on Wednesday nights, not the youth group. He was enjoying that time with Amber. He knew by next year as a youth ministry major, he would be expected to become involved with a youth program, but this year he didn't have to, and he had liked the idea of doing something he hadn't done before and he knew Amber enjoyed. She liked working with older kids too, but this was more physically demanding than emotional, and after a summer of counseling, they both had needed a break from that type of ministry.

Seth was glad to see Josiah join them for dinner in the cafeteria also. He had invited him earlier today when he left the room to go spend time with Amber, and he'd been trying to include Josiah. He didn't know a lot of other people here, and he didn't have a girlfriend like his three roommates did.

Seth hoped that would be changing soon. Josiah had asked his sister out, and he had a good feeling about it. He thought Josiah was a lot like Dylan, only more like Dylan used to be than he was now. He had no doubt Kerri would bring out the best in him if this turned into more than one date.

"Where's Kerri tonight?" Chad asked. He was sitting across from him, and Seth started to answer, but Blake beat him to it.

"Out with Kevin."

"Kevin who?"

"From Tony's? Kevin, Kevin."

"Oh," he said, appearing confused. Seth stepped in to clarify. Blake made it sound like it was a date. With Josiah sitting right there, he didn't want him to get the wrong impression.

"She went to his piano recital."

"And dinner," Blake said.

Seth didn't comment. Blake knew Kevin and his family better than he did, so he supposed Blake was excited someone new was going to hear him play.

"How good is he, Blake?" Seth asked. "Really?"

"Really?" Blake laughed. "Pretty stinkin' good. You've got to go sometime."

"We thought about it, but Kerri said we need to be invited. How do we get invited?"

Blake smiled. "It's okay if you want to show up sometime, but if you want to get invited—I don't know. Kevin invites who he wants to invite. It took him two years to invite me."

"How did Kerri get invited? She's known him for a month."

Blake laughed. "I think Tony had a hand in that, but the dinner thing—there's only one explanation, and you're definitely not getting asked for that reason."

Seth felt completely lost. "What reason?"

Everyone else at the table seemed as intrigued by Blake's words as he was, but Jessica leaned over and said something to Blake the rest of them couldn't hear, and then he sobered a bit and said, "Maybe you should talk to Kevin about it. I wouldn't want to be putting words into his mouth. It's Kevin. Most of us only understand what he does half the time."

Seth saw Jessica glance at Josiah, appearing strangely uncomfortable with this conversation, and it was then he caught on to what Blake was saying. Kerri might not know it, but she was on a date with Kevin. Then again, maybe she did, considering the way she had been all fixed up. But why would she agree to go out with Josiah if she liked Kevin? That wasn't like her.

He let it go for now, and later when he asked Amber if she knew anything different than what Kerri had said about tonight, she said she didn't, but she thought Jessica must know something by the way she had spoken to Blake. He thought about saying something to Josiah when he returned to the room, but he decided he would leave any explaining up to Kerri. He didn't know what was going on. The only thing he knew for sure was when he walked Amber up to her room at 9:55, Kerri wasn't back yet.

***

Lauren was wondering how Kerri's evening with Kevin and his family was going on the drive back to campus. After working a full day at Tony's, she was tired, but Saturdays were actually her favorite day of the week. She enjoyed working more than attending classes and studying. The work itself was fun, the environment positive, and the perk of getting free pizza for lunch and dinner was nice.

Seeing Adam all day was the best part. He was back to his normal self, and other than giving her a hug first thing this morning and apologizing again for last night, neither of them had mentioned it, and their day had taken its usual course. Kerri wasn't with them on the drive back, but she wasn't thinking about that aspect until Adam made a special point of saying something when they reached the campus.

"Can I ask you to do something, Angel?"

"Sure," she replied.

Adam was looking for a parking spot, and he made his request before he pulled into one. "Whenever we're alone after dark, like tonight, don't sit in the truck with me once we arrive at our destination. If I don't get out right away, then you get out, okay?"

"Okay."

He parked the truck and shut off the engine. She was used to him getting out first and coming to open the door for her. It wasn't something she expected him to do, but he had always done so since the first time he had taken her out for pizza. A few times he had remained in the truck, and they had spent some time talking and kissing, like last night—only that had turned into something more.

When he didn't get out right away this time, she caught on he was testing her. She laughed and opened her own door, and when he came around to meet her, he thanked her seriously.

"I'll try and not make you do that, but if you ever need to, don't hesitate, okay?"

She nodded. She didn't speak because a lump was rising in her throat. She had appreciated Adam's apology this morning, but she needed more than to hear him say he was sorry. She needed a solution to the problem, and this told her he wasn't leaving it all up to her.

"Come on, let's walk a little," he said, taking her hand and leading her to a pathway that would end in front of her dorm but gave them a few more minutes than walking straight there.

On the way he told her about talking to Seth last night and having more practical solutions he wanted to talk to her about, but he didn't want to get into it all tonight. They were both tired, and he said tomorrow would be better. She accepted that and didn't feel like saying good-night to him yet, but he thought it would be best, so she didn't argue.

He gave her a hug instead of kissing her, and she was okay with that too. She actually needed it more than a kiss, and she got the feeling Adam did also.

"You mean the world to me, Lauren. I promise to take better care of you from now on."

"You don't have to do it all yourself," she said. "I'll help however I can. I want us to take care of each other."

He didn't say anything else, but he held her tighter.

"Thank you for talking to Seth. That means a lot to me. I'm sure it wasn't easy."

"You're worth it, Angel. I would do anything for you."

"For us," she corrected him. "You need this as much as I do, Adam."

***

Stepping into the cool evening air outside the concert hall, Kerri saw Kevin waiting for her, but he was talking to someone. She approached them, and when Kevin spotted her, he shifted his attention from the short, older gentleman, and they both turned to face her.

"Professor Douglas, this is Kerri," Kevin said.

"Hello, Kerri. Good to meet you," he said, shaking her hand. "I've been teaching Kev piano since he's been at Humboldt, and I've never heard him play like he played tonight."

"That's what I heard," she said. "I guess I came on the right night."

He chuckled. "Yes, I'd say so. I'll let you two get to dinner," he said, turning to shake Kevin's hand and slapping his upper arm at the same time. "Great job, Kevin. See you on Monday."

"Thank you, Professor. Have a good night."

Once the professor stepped away, Kerri looked back to Kevin and smiled. It hadn't been just the two of them since this afternoon at the park, and she waited for him to take the lead here. One thing she had noticed about him was that he often let others speak for him, but if she gave him the opportunity to speak for himself, he did unless he didn't have anything to say, and she couldn't imagine that being the case right now.

He stepped forward and took her hands, holding them thoughtfully before speaking. "You remember how I said when I'm with you, I feel different?"

"Yes."

"I felt that tonight when I was playing. I don't do that."

"Do what?"

"Feel anything when I'm playing. It's just notes and keys to me, but tonight it was music."

"It was really beautiful," she said. "Were you playing for me?"

"No, I was playing for me, but I was thinking of you."

She smiled. She knew Kevin had no idea he had said one of the most romantic things she'd ever heard.

"And what were you thinking about me?" she asked, squeezing his hands and tilting her chin up a bit when he took a step closer.

"That you're beautiful and you make my heart happy and I like being with you."

"And I'm really good at making pizza?"

"No," he said, leaning his forehead against hers. "You're silly."

"I know," she said, holding her breath at his closeness, but she didn't feel uncomfortable or threatened by it.

"Hey, Kevin!" she heard someone say behind her.

He lifted his eyes and backed away, but he didn't let go of her hands. "Hey, Damien," he said. "Good job tonight."

Kerri turned to see the college student who was also dressed in a tuxedo. "I did all right, but you rocked, man. Where did that come from? You been taking private lessons this summer behind Professor Douglas' back?"

"No. I just felt it tonight. Tonight it was music."

"You've got that right," he said, slapping him on the shoulder. "And who's this?"

"This is Kerri," he said, stepping away so Damien could introduce himself but only letting go of one of her hands. Damien took the other one and gave her a kiss on the back of her fingers. She could tell right off that Damien was a ladies' man, but she greeted him politely and felt protected by Kevin's presence, and Damien obviously knew Kevin's plans.

"You taking her to dinner with you?"

"Yes, I am," he said. "We'd better go, or we're going to be late."

"Can't have that," Damien said, laughing mildly. "Great job tonight, Kev. I hope to hear more of that in the future. And good night, Kerri. It was nice meeting you."

"Nice meeting you," she echoed.

Damien stepped away, and Kevin turned them toward the parking lot without letting go of her hand. "My dad said you should drive your car back to the pizza place, and then we can go from there. They might close the gate here, and it will be safer there anyway. He told me I should have picked you up at school, but I didn't think of that."

"That's all right," she said.

"I'll do that next time."

"Okay," she said, not feeling the need to inquire about when that might be. "But it was worth the drive. You really did play beautifully. Do you ever play anyplace besides school?"

"I play at church on Sunday nights for the worship band. I play keyboard though. It's different than how I play at school."

"Oh, I think I knew that," she said, remembering her new plans to start attending that service. She had gotten her work schedule at The Oasis changed to not working Sunday nights and working every other Monday instead. "That's why you need Seth to work on Sundays."

"Yes. That's why. We need someone good on Sundays. It's a busy night."

He walked with her to the car and said he would meet her at Tony's. She got in and made her way there, thinking about Josiah for part of the journey. She knew their time together tomorrow was going to be different than she had been imagining the last couple of days, but she didn't feel she was doing anything wrong by letting things progress with Kevin. When she had agreed to have lunch with Josiah, she hadn't realized how this night could turn out, and she had been doing it as a friend. She wanted to hear the story that had gotten Josiah here and give him any advice or insight she could. And at this point, she knew that's all she would be doing tomorrow.

Getting out of her car after she had parked at Tony's, she saw Kevin get out of his, and she walked that way. It wasn't until then she realized the red VW Bug she had seen parked here belonged to Kevin. She wanted one just like it.

"I love your car," she said. "How long have you had it?"

"Three years," he said.

She was surprised because it looked brand new from the outside, and the inside was spotless too. She thanked him when he opened the door for her, and she slipped inside. Kevin didn't talk to her as he drove out of the parking lot and onto the main street heading out of town, seeming to need to focus completely on his driving, so she didn't interrupt him and enjoyed the quiet.

The restaurant was a little ways up the coast, and it was still light enough when they arrived to see the beautiful view of the Pacific Ocean from the large windows of the small dining area where they were seated. It was a large restaurant, but it was divided into a lot of little rooms to give it a cozy feel. She sat beside Kevin, and Jenna was on her other side, and she wondered if it felt strange to the others to have her there, but no one said anything about the change in routine.

They all raved about Kevin's performance at first, but then Kerri found a lot of the attention being focused on her. His mom hadn't heard her telling

Jenna about herself, so she got to share all that over again. His parents reminded her of her own in a lot of ways. They asked about her family, and she enjoyed telling them about her brothers and older sister and her parents.

"Are you missing them a lot?" Jenna asked after their salads were served.

"Yes," she said, noticing Kevin didn't want any salad, but the waitress brought him more bread.

"Having my brother here helps. I'm sure I would be missing everyone a lot more if he wasn't."

Jenna had an understanding look on her face, and Kerri supposed Jenna and Kevin were very close. They acted like it, and she could imagine Jenna always doing everything she could to watch out for him and be there for whatever he needed, perhaps to the point of having to sacrifice some of her own plans.

When she finished eating her salad, Kevin leaned over and asked if she wanted to dance. She could tell he was getting tired of sitting. He didn't like to sit in one place for too long, even when he took a break for dinner at the pizza place. He would eat really fast and then go play pinball or go outside for the rest of the time, so she knew he wasn't here so much for the food.

She smiled and said she would love to. He led her to another room where piano music was being played and there was a small dance floor. It overlooked the ocean, but it was mostly dark outside now. She could see a lighthouse beam in the distance and the outline of cliff rocks above the water, but that was all.

"I'm not a great dancer," she warned him, leaning into his arms and taking simple steps.

"Me neither," he said. "I just want to hold you close to me."

She leaned her head against his shoulder and relaxed in his arms. She loved his simplicity and honesty. He might not always know how to connect with people or what to say, but he was giving her exactly what she needed.

"I like you holding me," she said. "And you can do it anytime, not just when we're dancing, okay?"

"Okay," he said.

When they returned to the table, their entrées had been served, and she noticed Kevin's simple platter compared to the rest. He had ordered off the menu like they all had, and he had ordered the same thing as his mom, but their plates looked very different. His mom's chicken and pasta had cream sauce all over it, and the vegetables were mixed and decoratively arranged. But Kevin's chicken was totally plain with no sauce, he had a scoop of macaroni and cheese beside it, and instead of mixed vegetables, he only had carrots.

"Does that look all right, Kevin?" the waitress asked when she came over to check on them.

"Yes, it's fine," he said.

Kerri knew the people here must know Kevin's picky tastes well. At the pizza place he always made himself the same kind of pizza for dinner—pan crust with only sauce and pineapple; no cheese, no meat, nothing but pineapple. She had asked him about it one time, and he said, "This is how I like it."

Leaning over and teasing him a bit tonight, she said, "Is that what you always have here?"

"No. Sometimes I have fruit instead of carrots."

"What kind of fruit, pineapple?"

Jenna heard her say that, and she laughed. "Or grapes," she interrupted. "Right, Kev?"

Kevin seemed to catch on they were teasing him. "I like grapes," he said.

She learned something after dinner she hadn't realized before. When they went to get in their separate cars, Jenna asked him what time he thought he would be home, and Kevin gave her a definite time. After they were inside the car, Kerri asked him what she suspected.

"Do you live with Jenna?"

"Yes. We have an apartment by the school."

"How long have you lived with her?"

"Five years, since I started going to Humboldt."

"Do you like it?"

"Yes."

"What are you going to do when she gets married next summer?"

He didn't answer that, and she sensed his agitation. She suddenly realized no one had talked of Jenna's fiancé during dinner, and Jenna had only mentioned him that one time before the concert.

Kevin backed out of the parking space and didn't speak once they were on the highway, but she knew his silence had more to do with her question about Jenna than him needing to concentrate. When she saw a sign for a beach access area along the highway she had been to before, she asked Kevin if they could stop and take a walk, and he pulled off the road. She wanted to ask him something, but she didn't want him to be distracted while he was driving.

There had been one time a few weeks ago when something had gone wrong in the kitchen and she had seen his autism limiting his ability to handle it calmly. He had gotten very frustrated, and everyone got out his way for a few moments like they'd seen it before.

He hadn't been angry or threatening to anyone, just unable to function in a rational and cooperative way until his dad came back and calmed him down. He ended up going outside, and when he came back he was perfectly fine. When she'd said that about his sister, she had seen that same look on his face he'd had that day. It had gone away, but he had never answered the question.

They were dressed too nicely to go for a walk on the beach like she really wanted to, but there was a little pathway with a railing overlooking the waves. They walked to the end, and they were both quiet until she spoke.

"Are you upset that Jenna's getting married?"

He didn't say anything. She didn't think he was going to answer her and wondered if he had totally closed himself off. She reached for his hand and held it gently. Her touch seemed to break through his state of mind.

"I don't like it," he finally said.

"Why?" she asked.

"I just don't."

"Is it because you don't like the guy she's marrying or because—"

"I don't like it, Kerri. I don't want to talk about it."

She remained silent, wondering if she should let it go for now and change the subject, or wait to see if he would say something. She decided to wait.

He kept staring out at the water, and she knew she had lost the connection she'd had with him ever since this afternoon. But she had an unexplainable sense of peace. *Be still and know that I am God.* She chose to do so in that moment.

About ten seconds later, he started to cry, and it broke her heart. It wasn't like the way a grown man cried in a moment of brokenness. It was like the way a little boy cried when he got scared or hurt or lost his mommy in the store.

She stepped into his arms, and he clung to her. She let him cry, and when he spoke, it made her start crying too. He had the most tender heart she had ever known. She thought her dad and Seth had tender hearts, but this was in another realm of emotions—like a little boy and grown man at the same time. Like a teenager who wasn't afraid to show how needy and helpless he felt.

"I don't want anything to change," he said. "I don't like it. I don't want it."

He had taken off his jacket before they'd gone into the restaurant, and he hadn't put it back on when they got out of the car; he had given it to her. She didn't know if he was shaking because of cold or his emotions, but he was definitely shivering. Taking off the jacket, she wrapped it around his shoulders instead.

The warmth seemed to calm him, and she waited for him to say more, but when he didn't, she decided to say what she was thinking. If he got upset again, she would suggest they go and leave this discussion for another time—if ever. Maybe she wasn't the one who should be doing this. She had known him for six weeks. His family had known him his whole life, and this wasn't about her, it was about Jenna.

"Kevin?"

"What?"

"Do you want Jenna to be happy?"

"Yes."

"Do you think she's happy with—what's his name?"

"Caleb."

"Do you think she's happy with Caleb?"

"Yes. They love each other."

She paused and then asked him something else. "Do you think you might like to get married someday and live with someone besides your sister?"

He got an embarrassed look on his face, and she smiled. He smiled back in a shy way, but he didn't say anything.

"You don't think it will ever happen for you, do you?"

"No."

She smiled gently, lifted her hand to his face, and caressed his smooth cheek. "It could happen," she said.

He didn't respond with words, but she could see the acceptance of his sister's future and the hope for his own filling his eyes. She had absolutely no idea why, but she knew his family was right about her having an ability to reach his heart in a way others couldn't. And the closer she got, the closer she wanted to be.

She kept her hand on his face and kissed him gently on the lips. He remained perfectly still for a moment, but when she didn't kiss him again, he searched for her lips, and he kissed her in an extremely innocent but highly affectionate way.

She got lost in his touch. He made her feel like she was very precious to him, and it convinced her she wanted this. Kevin wasn't like anyone she had ever imagined being with, but she wanted it. She wanted him.

"I love you, Kerri," he whispered, burying his face in her cheek and hair.

She never would have imagined herself saying so to any guy on their first date, but she did.

"I love you too, Kevin."

Chapter Nineteen

Lauren tried to stay awake and wait up for Kerri to return from her evening with Kevin, but by ten-thirty she couldn't keep her eyes open any longer and fell asleep. Colleen didn't even make it that long, but Amber was wide awake when she heard Kerri come in at eleven-thirty. Normally she would have let her be, but Seth had been worried about her and told her to call him if she wasn't back by midnight, so she used that cover-story to get the scoop on Kerri's evening.

Walking quietly into the other room, she saw Jessica was asleep too. She gave Kerri a hug and spoke in a whisper. "Is everything all right? Seth was worried about you."

Kerri smiled. "I'm fine. I didn't realize how late it was."

Amber heard the joy in Kerri's voice and saw a look of elation and wonder on her face. "How was it?" she asked.

"Really nice. Amazing." She laughed softly. "Unbelievable."

Amber smiled. "What's that mean?"

Kerri sighed and reached for her hands, pulling her over to the bed like they were in sixth grade at a slumber party and she had a really big secret to tell her. She took a deep breath and blurted it out in a loud whisper.

"I'm falling in love, Amber."

She said it with such peace and certainty, Amber could only smile, and she asked the only thing that made sense. "With Kevin?"

She nodded. "Yes," she said. "Don't ask me how or why exactly, but I am."

Amber felt speechless. "Wow. Did all of this happen tonight, or have you been holding out on us?"

"I think it's been happening for awhile, but I didn't realize it until today."

Jessica stirred in her sleep, and Amber didn't want to wake her, but this was too huge to wait and hear the rest tomorrow.

"What happened?"

Kerri told her what Lauren had said about Kevin inviting her to dinner, how she had seen Kevin at the park this afternoon and what he'd said about her making him feel different, and how he played tonight and Kevin and his family saying it was because of her.

"His mom said to me, 'You've reached a part of his heart no one else can,' and at first I freaked out and felt like I had to get out of there, but then when I saw Kevin and he held me so tight, I knew he wasn't the only one who was feeling something."

"And after that?"

"I just let it happen. Like I would if it was any other guy I really liked. I was completely myself, and he let me be that way. We danced three times, and I had goose bumps each time. We stopped at the beach on our way back, and we talked, and he told me personal things that were hard for him to say, and then I kissed him and he kissed me back!"

Amber smiled and had tears in her eyes. Kerri didn't do this over guys. She didn't kiss guys freely or let them kiss her until she was good and ready, but Amber knew that feeling of everything clicking and being in the middle of something she knew she wanted but hadn't been able to imagine beforehand.

"How does this compare to what you had with Dylan?"

"I was thinking about that on the drive back. It's the same in terms of knowing what's happening is what I want, but it's different because I chose Dylan, and I knew he was a safe choice. But Kevin is choosing me, and it's not safe. It's good, but not safe."

"What do you mean?"

She laughed. "I'm dating a guy I don't understand! I can't even begin to figure him out. I can't go down my checklist and say, 'He's that and that and that.' I can in a way. Kevin meets all the things I'm looking for—the stuff I can't bend on—but then there's all this other stuff I don't have a category for."

"But it's good?"

"Yes. I can't explain it, but in my heart I know it's good."

Amber gave her a hug. "I'm happy for you."

"Thanks," she said. "And don't wait for me in the morning. I'm going to hang out here and then go to the service at six. I got my work schedule changed."

"Does Kevin go to that one?"

"Yes, he plays the keyboard." She laughed. "Although, that's not why I originally decided to go. But that's another story. I'll tell you later."

"Okay," Amber said. "Good night."

"Good night."

Kerri was still sleeping when she and Colleen left the room in the morning, so she told Seth what she knew at breakfast, and they went to church in town without Kerri this time. She knew Josiah usually went to the service held on Sunday evenings too, and she suspected that may have been Kerri's original reason for switching. That's what Seth thought too, and he didn't sound disturbed by Kerri's choice to allow something to begin with Kevin instead, but he seemed curious.

"You hate you have no part of this, don't you?" she asked after they saw Kevin at church. He was one of the greeters at the front door, and he was always friendly and welcoming, but he didn't treat them differently than normal, and he didn't ask about where Kerri was, so Amber knew she must have told him she wouldn't be here.

"Yeah, pretty much," Seth said, laughing mildly. "I'm sure she knows what she's doing, I just wish I did."

"She's a big girl, Seth. And she's waited on God for this. I know you haven't seen her since yesterday, but I did, and she was completely at peace when she was telling me about it. You were telling me last weekend about how unsettled she seems, remember?"

"Yes."

"Well, trust me. She wasn't like that last night. She knows exactly what she's doing."

They found some seats, and he let out a heavy sigh, but he took her hand and said, "You mean like I knew what I was doing when I kissed you on your sixteenth birthday and asked you to be my girlfriend?"

"Yes. Just like that."

He gave her a light kiss and seemed to relax a bit. "And when I asked you to marry me this summer and you said yes?"

"Yes. If we can be young and crazy, so can she."

"I knew it was all going to come back and haunt me: When I broke our pact; When I found myself falling in love with you; When I bought that ring—"

"Are you getting a sense of how my dad and brother have been feeling for the last two years?"

He smiled.

"You want to know a secret?" she asked.

"What?"

"With as concerned as they were about me, and with all they did to try to protect and watch out for me, it still came down to me making the right choices for myself. I didn't want to ever have to hide anything from my family or disappoint them, but mostly I made the right choices for me, not them."

Seth didn't respond, but she knew he understood what she was saying.

"Kerri knows what she wants, Seth. Trust her on this, okay?"

"Okay," he said, kissing her on the cheek and pulling her close to him. "If you can trust me, I can trust her."

***

When Kerri opened her eyes at ten-thirty, she knew she was alone because it was quiet. She had been wakened a few times already by her roommates getting ready for church, but she had remained in bed because if she got up, everyone would be asking her questions about last night, and she didn't want that yet. She had enjoyed sharing with Amber, but otherwise she wanted to keep it to herself for now. Falling in love wasn't something she did every day.

She took a shower and got dressed for her lunch-date with Josiah. She spent the remaining minutes before she needed to leave rereading her devotional for yesterday and the things she had written in her prayer journal before Kevin had pleasantly interrupted her. She wanted to read it for two reasons: One, because she didn't have time to do another full lesson right now; and two, because she couldn't remember exactly what the lesson had been about or what she had gotten out of it. She often did that before going on to the next one, but today the review from yesterday was enough for today also. She could go for months on it.

It had been about faith and giving things to Jesus. In the Bible story where Jesus feeds more than 5000 people from a young boy's small lunch, the disciples were given instructions to feed them on their own, but when they didn't have enough faith to do so, Jesus said, "Bring the food to me." They gave the bread and fish to Jesus and He multiplied it and gave it back to the disciples to give the food to the people.

One of the questions in the study said: *What are some current challenges or circumstances you need to give over to Jesus?*

Kerri had listed a lot of things regarding her current life and her future. At the bottom of her list she had written: *Kevin?*

She remembered not being sure if that was something she should be concerned about or not. But last night she had taken her limited understanding about Kevin and given it over to Jesus. It had been one thing to write his name in a journal, and quite another to actually live it when she was in the middle of an unexpected turn of events with undeniable things going on in her heart, but she had, and she was so glad.

She could have run last night and totally missed it, or she could have tried to handle everything herself and made a mess of it, but she had simply surrendered herself to God's care and Kevin's open heart, and the outcome had been amazing.

She smiled at the thought of kissing him last night. She was the only girl he had ever kissed, but he didn't kiss like it had been his first time. They had been gentle, loving, and innocent, but not awkward or uncomfortable. Surprising yet perfect; that's how she would describe them.

She had underlined one phrase in the study in the closing paragraph, and she read it once again, allowing the truth of it to sink into her heart on this day-after a perfect date. *Giving things over to Jesus is an act of faith, and Jesus will prove His faithfulness to you one way or another.*

She had experienced His faithfulness last night, and she had to believe she would experience the same today: when she met Josiah for lunch and informed him of her rapid change of heart since seeing him two days ago; and when she saw Kevin later tonight. She had this little fear he would shut down toward her after being so open yesterday, either a little bit or a lot, but she prayed that wouldn't happen. She knew she wanted this, and she believed Kevin did too.

She had planned to meet Josiah downstairs at noon, and when she saw him waiting outside for her, she could see a look on his face indicating he knew something was up. She wondered how much of this he'd already heard, but she wanted to be completely honest with him. He may have been a good choice, but God had brought her together with the perfect choice at just the right time.

Chapter Twenty

Seeing Kerri coming out the front door of Priscilla Hall, Josiah smiled at her, and he knew right away she was either extremely happy to see him or she'd had a very nice time with Kevin last night. He didn't know exactly who Kevin was. He knew he worked at Tony's with Seth, Adam, and Chad, but they hadn't talked about him until last night at dinner. He had expected Seth to say something more about it when he got back to the room last night, but when Seth didn't, he knew something was going on he felt he should hear from Kerri.

"Hi," Kerri said with a bit of a sigh. She appeared to want to blurt out whatever it was, but she waited for him to return the greeting.

"Good morning," he said. "You look happy."

She smiled. "That's because I am."

"And why is that?"

"Can we talk before we go eat, or are you starving?"

"I'm all right," he said. "What's up?"

She sat beside him on the edge of the raised flowerbed. "First of all, I want you to know when I agreed to meet you for lunch today, I honestly wanted to hear your story and have time with you. You're the first guy I've felt that way about since I broke up with Dylan two months ago, and there wasn't anyone before him, so I do think you're a really special guy I could take a chance on dating."

"But?"

"But, something unexpected happened yesterday I need to tell you. I do still want to hear your story today if you want to tell me, but I'm not going to be considering this a date."

"Because you're dating Kevin?" he guessed.

"Yes. Did Seth tell you?" she asked, sounding apologetic.

"Not really. They were talking about you going out with him last night, and Seth was making it sound like it was a friend-thing, but Blake seemed to be thinking of it more like a date."

"Blake was right, but I didn't know that until yesterday," she laughed. "Which is why Seth didn't know either. And if you don't believe me, you can ask him, because I usually tell him everything."

"I believe you," he said, feeling disappointed this wasn't going to be what he had been hoping for, but not too devastated. In a way he felt relieved because he wasn't sure dating his roommate's sister would be too good of an idea, even if, or maybe especially because Seth thought the world of her. "What happened?"

"Have you ever met Kevin?"

"I don't think so."

"He plays the keyboard at church on Sunday nights."

"Oh? That Kevin? Yeah, I've met him. I didn't realize he was the same Kevin who worked at Tony's."

"He's Tony's son, and I met him the first weekend here. I don't know what compelled me to do such a thing, but I asked him if I could watch him make pizza, and then I helped him that night and every Saturday since."

"But you weren't interested in him?"

"No. I thought he was sweet, and I liked having that time with him, but I honestly didn't think much about it until this week after I accepted his invitation to his recital and dinner with his family, and then I found out from Lauren that's a huge step for him."

She went on to talk about him for ten minutes or more, and Josiah knew Kerri wasn't fooling around. She cared for Kevin and thought the world of him. Josiah felt happy for her and also for Kevin. He could imagine Kerri radically changing his life from something good and happy to something he'd never had the capacity to imagine.

"Anyway, I'm babbling," she said, not appearing the least bit sorry. "Do you still want to have lunch with me, or have I totally ruined your day?"

He laughed. "I'm not sure it's possible for you to ruin anyone's day, Kerri. And honestly, I'm happy for you. I'm afraid my story is going to be very depressing compared to that."

"Do you want to eat now and then tell me afterwards? I'm free all afternoon."

"Sure."

They walked to the cafeteria, and he told her things about himself as she began asking him lots of questions. He asked her some in return, and by the time they were finished eating, he felt comfortable telling her about Gabe. She wasn't the type of person who would say, 'What a jerk. Just stop being his friend and forget about it.'

Their space was invaded by those returning from church, so he decided to wait until they were alone again. Seth and Amber found them sitting there, and he could tell Seth was anxious to talk to his sister, but he accepted her promise to meet him later.

"Don't worry, it's good," she said, giving him a hug. "How about if I meet you at three?"

"Okay," he said. "At The Oasis?"

"That's fine," she said.

Josiah left with Kerri, and he had a different feeling than he'd ever had with a girl before. He was getting to know her, but without the pressure of having to decide if they wanted to take this beyond friendship. He had wanted that with other girls but always had a difficult time getting there.

Kerri seemed to be an expert on being friends with a guy, however, and as he spilled his story that was heavy on his heart, she listened well, and he became more thankful by the minute this wasn't a date because he felt more free to talk about it like he knew he really needed to.

***

Listening to Josiah share about his friend from back home, Kerri was reminded of Matt. Gabe's mistakes were more serious, but he had a friend who cared about him like Seth had cared about Matt and never given up on him.

Gabe and Josiah had been friends since junior high, and Josiah knew he was the quiet one and more of a follower. Gabe was more social. He had been dating girls since he was fourteen and was a natural-born leader. For the most part Josiah saw him as being a good friend and an all-around good guy. He hadn't gotten caught up in the party scene, drinking, or drugs like some of their other friends. He was basically a good kid who got decent grades, came from a good family, and enjoyed life for what it was.

Between their junior and senior year, Gabe had gone to live with his grandparents in Oregon for the summer because his parents were going on a short-term mission trip and they didn't want him to be home alone for eight weeks. He had a good relationship with his grandparents and had been happy to go and have that time with them. Josiah had gone down for a couple of weeks to spend time with him there. One of those weeks they had gone to Camp Laughing Water together, and they'd had a lot of fun. Gabe had seemed solid spiritually that week, more so than Josiah had ever known him to be, and Gabe had also met a girl during his time in Oregon who Josiah saw as being a positive influence on him.

Rachael attended the same church as Gabe's grandparents. They had gotten to know each other and by mid July were dating. She had been at camp with them that week also. Josiah had the chance to meet her and see everything Gabe had told him was true. She was beautiful and sweet, and she had a very solid relationship with God. At the end of the summer they decided they wanted to keep their relationship going on a long-distance basis, and Gabe had been serious about it, going to see her a couple of times that fall and keeping in contact with her consistently. As far as Josiah could tell, they were falling in love and they had a good relationship.

But after Valentine's Day, when he had gone to see Rachael once again, Gabe changed. He became more distant with him, and he started hanging out with a girl at their church. He kept saying they were just friends and he and Rachael were still together and everything was fine, but Josiah knew something wasn't right. Gabe began spending less time with him, talked less and less of Rachael, and eventually Josiah discovered Gabe had been spending time with Sienna and lying about it.

Josiah confronted him during Spring Break. He went on a camping trip with Gabe's family, and he saw a bunch of unopened letters from Rachael in Gabe's desk drawer when he was helping him look for his map of the Mt. Rainier Wilderness. Gabe had confessed he hadn't been opening her letters since he had gone to visit her in February because he felt like they had gotten too serious. But he hadn't told Rachael and was still calling her and acting like everything was fine.

"I asked him pointblank, 'Are you dating Sienna? Have you kissed her? What have you told her about Rachael?' And he told me they were dating, he had kissed her, and he had told Sienna he broke up with Rachael."

"But he hadn't?" Kerri asked.

"No."

"What did you tell him?"

"I told him if he didn't want to be with Rachael anymore that was his choice to make, but he needed to tell her the truth. He said he was going to, but when I asked him about it again, he said he wasn't sure if he wanted to: he liked them both and felt confused."

"Wow," Kerri said. "What did you say to that?"

"I wasn't sure what to do. I told him what I thought, but I couldn't force him to tell either Rachael or Sienna the truth, so I prayed about it and left him alone. I figured he would sort it out for himself, and with graduation coming up and our plans to go to Seattle Pacific together, maybe it would all blow over."

"I take it that didn't happen. Why did you end up here?"

Josiah's expression went from concern to complete downcast. "About a month after graduation Gabe called me and said Sienna was pregnant, but he didn't know if he was going to marry her. When I asked him about Rachael, he said he told her he couldn't see her later that month like they were planning because he was going into the Air Force."

"Did he enlist?"

"No. That was total lie. As we speak, Gabe is a student at Seattle Pacific, Sienna is in Bellingham thinking Gabe might want to marry her at some point, and Rachael believes he's off at some Air Force base and is waiting to hear from him so she can start writing to him again. I called him last night, hoping all that had changed, but it hasn't."

"Why are you here?"

"I couldn't deal with it anymore. He wasn't listening to me, and I couldn't sit by and watch him do it."

"What are you thinking now?"

"The only thing I have any control over is to tell Rachael the truth since Gabe won't do it. She's a sweet girl, and I can't believe he's doing this to her. That breaks my heart more than anything."

"Do you have a way of contacting her?"

"Yes, several. I'm trying to decide what would be the best way."

Kerri thought about how she would want to hear the news. There was no good way, she knew, but some were better than others.

"I'm thinking about sending her a letter in the mail. What do you think?"

"Good choice," she replied.

"Do you think I should tell her?"

"Yes."

"Will you help me write it? I don't know what to say."

"Yes, I will. I know it doesn't seem like it, but you're being a better friend to Gabe this way, and even if he never appreciates it, I know Rachael will."

***

With as good as Kerri felt about talking to Josiah, both in sharing her news about Kevin and listening to his story about Gabe, she felt considerably more unsure about talking to Seth as she went to meet him at The Oasis. She knew he had heard some of it from Amber already, but this wasn't just about the details of what had happened last night.

This was about things that had been going on in her heart for months concerning her relationship with God, and what had been happening in the last few weeks between herself and Kevin, but more so on a heart level than specific details she could share with him.

He was waiting for her when she arrived, and he was alone. If Amber had been there too, she would have felt less concerned with what she was going to say, but since it was just him, she knew he was looking for serious answers from her, which was fine. She would expect that from him but wasn't sure if she had the words to explain herself.

Seth gave her a hug and held on for a moment, and she found that comforting. He was in a supportive mood where he would listen more than talk. After living all those years as kids in their parents' house, it struck her they were grown up now and away at college on their own.

Neither of them were hungry, so they found an empty couch in the corner by the windows, and once she had removed her coat and got settled, she sighed and couldn't help but smile.

"How much have you already heard from Amber?"

"Some," he said. "Enough to know you think you're falling in love with Kevin and you let him kiss you."

"Yes, I did. Although, I actually kissed him first."

He smiled. "Why, Kerri? What were you thinking?"

She told him about Kevin being upset about Jenna, and then she explained how that fit in to all the other times she and Kevin had spent together.

"I can't explain it, Seth, but there's a connection between us neither of us are exactly sure how to find, but when we do, it's not something I want to let go of. It's not just about spending time together and having fun and talking and liking each other. I had that with Dylan, but I always felt like something was missing."

"Then you'd better watch out, because if it's anything like how I feel about Amber, you won't be able to let go."

"I think it might be," she laughed. "And consider this: One of the things I've been praying for is if I met a guy here, he would be someone you know well too. That's why I thought Josiah might be the right one, but instead of me dating your roommate, I'm dating your boss!"

He laughed. "That sounds like something God would do."

When Kerri got to church later, she knew she could use a good hug from Kevin, but she had to wait until she was finished with her girls' disciple group. At five-thirty, she went in search of him, knowing the band rehearsed in the multipurpose room where the worship gathering was held. Jessica was planning to stay since Chad was working tonight with Seth, but Kerri didn't wait for her to be finished with her own group. She wanted to see Kevin as soon as possible, and she wanted a couple of minutes alone with him.

She had enjoyed telling Seth about her time with Kevin and was glad he seemed happy for her, but Josiah's story had left her with a depressed feeling. She was glad he had talked to her, and she was fine with helping him write the letter, but she had seen this too many times.

Guys and girls from perfectly good Christian homes and churches ending up in ruins and hurting other people because they made stupid choices. They knew God but didn't live like it. She had been on that path

214

at one time too, and she was so thankful God had rescued her when He did, but she often felt clueless about how to show other people the right way. Sometimes they listened, sometimes they didn't. She knew Josiah was feeling that way about Gabe, and his heartbreak had become her own.

Kevin was standing at the keyboard on the wide stage when she entered the room. People were setting up the rest of the open area, and she wove her way around the temporary walls and chairs and was glad to see Kevin standing alone, but she had this little fear he wouldn't welcome her as easily as she needed him to right now.

Taking sheet music from a folder and placing it on the music stands, he caught sight of her, and an instant smile came to his face. She smiled in return, and he stepped over, giving her a nice hug without saying anything first.

"I missed you today," she said, feeling close to tears. It felt so good to have Kevin holding her in the same way he'd done last night. She had been feeling unsettled he would forget about the connection she had managed to find with him yesterday, and today she would be back to trying to find her way into his world. But he didn't seem to have forgotten anything.

"I missed you," he said and surprised her by kissing her right there in the middle of the bustling room. And it wasn't a quick kiss. His tender affection was the same as she had experienced last night. He made her feel very precious to him.

When he stopped, he was about to say something when whistles and shouts came from the middle of the room. One guy made a jungle-like noise and another said, "Way to go, Kevin!" She laughed and put her arms around his neck. Kevin laughed softly also, but he asked her for clarification.

"I'm sorry, was that bad?"

"No," she said. "They're just teasing you."

"I like kissing you," he said. "I've been waiting to do that all day."

"I like you kissing me," she said, looking into his eyes and giving him a light kiss. "You can kiss me anytime you want."

"Can I have time with you when this is over? I'm busy right now, but I won't be then."

"Will you drive me home tonight?"

"Yes, I can do that. I told Jenna I might be late."

"Like you were last night?"

He smiled. "Yes. But it was okay. She likes you."

"She told you that?"

"Yes."

"Did you say anything to her about what we talked about?"

"Yes. I told her."

"What did you say?"

"I said I wanted her and Caleb to get married and I would be all right without her. And I told her she could bring him to dinner after my next recital."

Kerri smiled, feeling amazed that Kevin would listen to her. "I'm proud of you."

"I feel better now."

She allowed him one more kiss and then went to find a seat to let him finish with setting up. He was on stage most of the time, and she sat with Jessica. The time of worship was uplifting, and she poured out her heart with gratitude to her faithful God who had brought such a special person into her life. She felt amazed with all that had happened in the past twenty-four hours, and in the middle of her happy moments, Josiah's story was a reminder that choosing God's way wasn't always easy, but it was always best.

The room had chairs in the main section, but there were several alcoves around the perimeter set aside for private prayer, journaling, communion, offering, and a place where they could submit prayer requests. They had done something similar at camp this summer, and one of the things she had always done during that time was to come alongside someone else who appeared to need extra support. At camp it had often been her camper girls, and some of her girls from her disciple group were here tonight, but they all seemed fine so she had private time with Jesus at the communion table during one of the songs and then went back to her seat.

She was pleasantly surprised when the pastor for this service said they were going to have fifteen minutes of quiet time where instead of loud music being sung and played, Kevin was going to be playing classical guitar for them, providing a soothing and meditative atmosphere to spend that time in reflection and prayer.

Since she had already had that for herself five minutes ago, she simply sat there and watched Kevin as he played the beautiful and soothing instrument that until now she didn't know he was also proficient in. She thought he was amazing. Like an onion with all these different layers for her to discover.

The only thing that distracted her from Kevin's playing was when she saw Josiah walk up to the front prayer benches. He knelt down and had only been praying for a minute when Kerri felt a strong leading to go and join him. He was crying, and she sat there silently and then prayed softly for him, for Gabe and Sienna, and for Rachael.

"This seems hopeless to us right now, Jesus. But we know You are able to take the most bleak situations and bad choices and bring grace and healing to these broken lives. I pray for Gabe and Sienna that they could turn back to you and be restored, and I pray for Rachael that as she receives this very difficult news, she would cling to you like never before and find what she can't find anywhere else: Peace—and in time, joy."

Chapter Twenty-One

Sunday evenings were normally relaxing for Adam. He worked at the cafeteria through dinner, but then he would meet Lauren and spend the rest of the evening with her. They didn't usually go into town because they worked a full day on Saturday and went back into town for church on Sunday mornings, had lunch there, and spent part of the afternoon together before he had to be back here to work.

He had decided to wait until tonight to tell her about Abby and what had been going through his mind on Friday night. He wanted to take a day to pray about it and make sure that's what he should do because he didn't want to hurt her in any way. God had confirmed it this morning at church and throughout the afternoon, and especially this evening when Abby had come into the cafeteria during dinner and made a special point to talk to him. He usually worked in the kitchen, not in the food service line, so he only saw people when he went out to replace one of the empty food bins. It was obvious she had been waiting to see him come out because she caught him during that brief span of time.

She said something about getting together with him sometime, and he told her he couldn't. "I'm really busy, Abby, and I try to spend all of my spare time with my girlfriend."

"I could meet her too," she said. "Maybe we could all have dinner sometime."

"I don't think that's a good idea."

"Why not?"

"I think you know why."

"That was a long time ago, Adam. We were young and did stupid stuff. Come on. I'll invite Elissa, and we'll laugh about that summer."

As he had backed into the kitchen, he felt determined to have the last word. "No, Abby. I can't."

That had been the easy part, now he had Lauren to face with the truth, but remembering what Seth had said about keeping their relationship sacred, he began talking with that mindset. The truth was sacred, lies and secrets were not.

***

Lauren listened as Adam told her about seeing Abby last week and how that had affected him in the days since then, especially on Friday night. She believed him when he said he had no real feelings for Abby and the thoughts in his mind had only surfaced because he hadn't taken any steps to keep them from doing so. She believed him because he was telling her about it when he didn't have to, and because he had talked to Seth. If he secretly wanted Abby instead of her, he would either tell her outright, or keep it a secret, not be telling her all the things he had done to try and keep this from breaking the sacredness of their relationship.

She liked how he talked about their relationship being sacred to him, and when he suggested they not spend time kissing in secluded places like his truck and elsewhere, she was fine with that. It hadn't been a problem for him before, but now it was. He also thought it would be good if they didn't see any movies for awhile, and she was okay with that too.

He apologized again for what had happened on Friday, and the brokenness in his voice told her he was having a much more difficult time forgiving himself than she had forgiving him. They had gone for a walk around the campus, and she stopped to give him a long hug.

"It's okay, Adam. It happened, and it's over, and I'm fine." Stepping back to look into his eyes, she continued. "What I don't want is for it to keep happening. I don't want to be battling it all the time. I don't want to be dreading our time together because I'm afraid of what might happen."

"I don't want that either, Angel. I've asked God for help, and I'm trusting He's going to do that, and I'm trying to take some steps to prevent it. *My* concern is that if I hold back on some of the affection I have in my heart for you, you'll start thinking I'm not feeling the same as before. And that's not true. I want to be with you. But I also care about you enough to know I need to take a step back right now."

"That's fine, Adam. I promise I won't think that."

He didn't say anything, but she could tell he was thinking something, and she asked him what it was.

"I'm thinking how thankful for you I am. Thankful you're not like Abby and trying to tempt me all the time, and thankful you're also willing to forgive me for messing up."

"And I'm thankful for you, Adam. You're being honest with me, and setting up these boundaries, and you aren't pressuring me to do things we shouldn't. I think there's a difference between getting caught up in the moment, and you trying to manipulate your way into something. You've never done that with me, and I don't believe you have that kind of heart."

He kissed her for the first time since Friday, and it was sweet. Just the way she liked them best. And after doing nothing but praying for Adam over the last two days, she knew those prayers had made a difference.

***

Josiah began to feel stronger as Kerri prayed, and he knew talking to her had been the right thing to do. Up until today he had felt alone in this. But he wasn't. He had Kerri's support and friendship, three great roommates he could count on, and Jesus to give him daily guidance and wisdom.

He liked Kerri's words about Gabe and Sienna finding healing and restoration in this, and for Rachael to find the strength to endure this difficult news and move on with her life by clinging to Jesus. He knew there was no easy way to say it, and with as much as she loved Gabe, he didn't feel it would be good for her to try and hang on to him. Gabe had serious decisions to make regarding Sienna and the baby, and even if he still loved Rachael, that was irrelevant now. He had made his choices, and he was going to have to live with them. Josiah only hoped Rachael wouldn't be too deeply scarred by his dishonesty and unfaithfulness.

He wrote the letter on Monday evening with Kerri's help, and he gave it to her to mail for him because he didn't know if he would have the courage. He tried to keep it simple and told Rachael to contact him if she needed to.

Two weeks later Rachael called him. It was Sunday afternoon, and he wasn't prepared for it. He thought she might the first week, but when she hadn't, he assumed she wouldn't, and the whole thing had slipped his mind over the last few days.

"Rachael, hi," he said, glancing at Seth who was getting ready to leave for work. "H-How are you?"

"Okay," she said, sounding lonely.

He turned away from Seth and gazed out the window, trying to decide how to respond. He wasn't great on the phone. "I'm really sorry, Rachael. I'm sorry I let this happen to you."

"You're sorry?" she said, sounding surprised. "Did you tell Gabe to cheat on me?"

"No, but I feel like I sat by and watched it happen. I didn't know—I tried to talk to him. I'm sorry."

"It's not your fault, Josiah, and you know what? I knew. I knew something was wrong, but I chose to ignore it. I didn't want to believe I was losing him, so I pretended that everything was fine, and I didn't confront him like I should have."

There was something he had been wondering about, and he'd asked Gabe but never gotten a straight answer. He decided to ask her.

"What happened back in February? He was different after that."

She didn't respond, and he backtracked.

"You don't have to tell me."

"No, it's okay. We talked about going to the same college, and I wanted that at first, but then he told me once we were in college he thought it would be all right if we started having sex because he knew he wanted to marry me someday. I didn't agree, and he said, 'You're going to make me wait until we're married? That might not be for another five years.' And I said, 'Yes. I'm not having sex with you until we're married. I made that commitment to myself a long time ago, and I'm not breaking it.' So by the time he left that weekend, he started talking about us getting married that summer, which I didn't want. Our weekend didn't end on a good note, but it wasn't like we broke up. I figured he would respect my wishes eventually, but I guess he couldn't live with that."

"I'm sorry," he said. "He never said anything to me about it, or I would have set him straight."

"It's not your fault, Josiah. And I appreciate you having the guts to tell me the truth. That's why I'm calling: to thank you." She changed the subject. "And, to find out what you're doing in California."

"I guess you could say Gabe isn't someone I wanted to be roommates with right now. After he lied to you about going into the Air Force, I said, 'That's it, Gabe. You're on your own. I'm not going to be a part of your lies anymore.' I wish I would have had the guts to call you then and spared you from three more months of waiting."

"Would you stop!" she laughed. "This is not your fault! I didn't call you to say, 'Why didn't you tell me sooner, or how could you let this happen?' I called to thank you and let you know I'm okay. Like I said, I already knew it was over. The pregnancy thing was pretty shocking, but on top of everything else, not that shocking."

"You're a nice girl, Rachael. I'm sorry this had to happen to you. I know you would have been good for Gabe. It's too bad he didn't realize how special you are."

"Thank you," she said. "At least I didn't throw my life away over him, right?"

"Right." He hesitated to ask the question on the tip of his tongue, but he did since she was being so honest. "Did you love him?"

"Yeah, I did. At least who he was in the beginning. I don't know if he changed or if that was never really him, but he filled a special place in my heart while it lasted."

"I think you saw who he could be, but he's kind of always ridden the fence, you know? God and church and everything is great until it starts to interfere with his life too much, and then he wants to pick and choose."

"Yeah, I saw signs of that sometimes too. I'm mad at him, but I'm also praying for him. If I'd only heard Gabe had been lying to me and had been seeing someone else, I think I would have been really hurt and mad, but when I heard he'd gotten some other girl pregnant, I felt sorry for him. I can cry a little and move on, but they can't. This is going to affect them for the rest of their lives."

They talked more, but not about Gabe. He asked how she liked college and found out about her current life. She was attending Oregon State University in her hometown, and she liked school, but she wasn't sure what she wanted to do. She had wanted to stay close to home and not move into the dorms this year, but she was thinking of doing that next year or possibly transferring to a Christian school. She asked about Lifegate, and he said he really liked it and she should check it out, and she said she might do that when she began looking more seriously.

Chad and Seth had left for work, and Adam was also gone. He found himself not wanting to say good-bye to her when it was obvious their conversation was coming to a close. He had a momentary thought about the two of them striking something up on a long-distance basis, but he dismissed it for several reasons: He supposed she wouldn't be anxious to go that route again; Dating his best friend's ex-girlfriend probably wouldn't help his relationship with Gabe; And Rachael was simply out of his league. Too pretty. Too perfect. She needed a better version of Gabe, not him.

"I just wanted to call and let you know I got the letter and to thank you," she said again. "I'll let you get back to whatever you were doing."

"I'm glad you called," he said. "I've been praying you would be all right, but it's nice to hear."

"You're sweet, Josiah. Would it be all right if I called you once in awhile? Just if I'm having a bad day or something?"

"That's fine."

"Thanks," she said. "And if you ever want to call me, like if you have an update on Gabe you think I might want to hear, feel free to do that. Do you have my number?"

"Yes. I got it from Gabe's phone when I was seriously thinking of calling you in July. I probably should—"

"Josiah! Stop!" She laughed.

"Okay, sorry."

They both laughed and then said good-bye to one another, but Josiah had the feeling he would be hearing from her again. And he hoped he was right.

***

Amber called home on Sunday night, and talking to her mom and dad had its usual result of mixed emotions after she hung up. It was good to touch base with them, share about her week, hear about theirs, and be reminded of their love, but she missed home. She missed her room and her friends and the predictability of life there. School had fallen into a routine, and her time with Seth was always pleasant. She knew she would rather see him every day here than be separated from him for days at a time there, but she wished she could have it all. All of the positive without any of the negative.

Feeling the need for an emotional boost with Seth working tonight, Kerri and Jessica in town, and Lauren out with Adam for the evening, she decided to call Mandy and caught her at home. She was usually home on Sunday nights because Matt had to be at youth group at Emmanuel, and her parents had a Bible study they went to, leaving her at home with Grandma. She missed her grandmother too and spent a few minutes chatting with her before she passed her over to Mandy.

"Hi, how are you?" she asked.

"I'm fine. How are you?"

"Missing home a little," she said. "What's the weather like there?"

"Raining, what else?"

"It's been raining here today too. I think it makes me miss home more."

"How's Seth?"

"He's fine. Slowly adjusting to the idea of his sister having a boyfriend."

"How's that going?" she asked. Amber had told her about it when she had called her two weeks ago.

"Great as far as I know. Kerri's actually been somewhat private about it. I think she's trying to keep it real between her and Kevin and not turn it into a source of the latest gossip, you know? They're really sweet together. Kevin is different with her than I've ever seen him with anyone else, and Kerri is different with him too, but neither of them are faking anything."

"Mmmm, that sounds like another couple I know."

"You and Matt?"

"Yes. People say that about us, and I know it's true."

"I'm one of them," she said. "I don't know if me and Seth are that way? What do you think?"

"Not so much," she said. "Although, I didn't know Seth before he knew you, and I didn't know you that well before you knew him. Someone like Stacey might see it differently."

"I need to call her. It's been a few weeks. Sometimes it seems like the weeks drag by but then I'm like, it's almost November? How can that be?"

"I know. Me too. Our six-month anniversary is coming up."

"Are you doing anything special?"

"Matt has something planned, but I don't know what it is."

"What a sweetheart."

"Yes, he is."

"Is he the one, Mandy?"

"The one what?"

She laughed. "The one you want to marry? Or do you know that yet?"

"I think he is," she said.

"How are things going with his family?"

"Okay. Not great. I still don't feel welcome there, but I think they've eased up on Matt. Pastor John has helped, and I do think it's good we stayed here. Matt has taken off spiritually even more than this summer. I feel like I can't keep up." She laughed. "He reminds me of you."

Amber smiled. That was good to hear. Mandy needed Matt to be the strong one. "I miss you guys. Both of you. I think me and Seth have connected better with you two than anyone else. Do you have anyone like that now?"

"Not really. Matt misses you both a lot. I do too, but he's said that several times."

"Maybe next year? Do you think?"

"Us being down there, you mean?"

"Yes."

"I don't know. Maybe. I know we'd like to be, but we're kind of waiting on God for that."

"And you should," she said. "But that's not gonna stop me from hoping for it."

"Do you feel ready to get married next summer?"

"Yes. But it seems a little unreal. It's hard to imagine right now, but I'm excited. I'm looking forward to the days when Seth has to get up early or comes home late but I still get to see him. It's funny how the more time I have with him, the more I want."

"I feel that way too," Mandy said. "After not seeing Matt for six days straight each week this summer, you would think I'd be happy with seeing him almost every day, and I was at first, but I'm missing him tonight."

"You were missing him two weeks ago too," she laughed.

"I know. You want to hear something crazy?"

"What?"

"I could marry him next summer too."

"That's not crazy, Mandy. Seeing Seth as little as I did for the first two years kept us moving at a steady pace, but since we've been here, it's taken us to a different level."

"And Matt and I have just gotten there sooner?"

"It's possible."

"I'm not going to be pushing Matt into anything, but if he feels that way too, I wouldn't be opposed to it."

"Does that mean I can start praying?"

Mandy laughed. "Yes, but don't tell Matt I said that."

"I won't. It will be our little secret. Just you, me, and Jesus. Matt won't know what hit him."

"Actually, with the way he's been lately, I wouldn't be surprised if he's the one who's been praying, and I won't know what hits me."

brought such a special person into her life. She felt amazed with all that had happened in the past twenty-four hours, and in the middle of her happy moments, Josiah's story was a reminder that choosing God's way wasn't always easy, but it was always best.

The room had chairs in the main section, but there were several alcoves around the perimeter set aside for private prayer, journaling, communion, offering, and a place where they could submit prayer requests. They had done something similar at camp this summer, and one of the things she had always done during that time was to come alongside someone else who appeared to need extra support. At camp it had often been her camper girls, and some of her girls from her disciple group were here tonight, but they all seemed fine so she had private time with Jesus at the communion table during one of the songs and then went back to her seat.

She was pleasantly surprised when the pastor for this service said they were going to have fifteen minutes of quiet time where instead of loud music being sung and played, Kevin was going to be playing classical guitar for them, providing a soothing and meditative atmosphere to spend that time in reflection and prayer.

Since she had already had that for herself five minutes ago, she simply sat there and watched Kevin as he played the beautiful and soothing instrument that until now she didn't know he was also proficient in. She thought he was amazing. Like an onion with all these different layers for her to discover.

The only thing that distracted her from Kevin's playing was when she saw Josiah walk up to the front prayer benches. He knelt down and had only been praying for a minute when Kerri felt a strong leading to go and join him. He was crying, and she sat there silently and then prayed softly for him, for Gabe and Sienna, and for Rachael.

"This seems hopeless to us right now, Jesus. But we know You are able to take the most bleak situations and bad choices and bring grace and healing to these broken lives. I pray for Gabe and Sienna that they could turn back to you and be restored, and I pray for Rachael that as she receives this very difficult news, she would cling to you like never before and find what she can't find anywhere else: Peace—and in time, joy."

Chapter Twenty-Two

Kerri was really happy to hear Rachael had called Josiah. She had been praying for that. She knew this kind of news could be devastating for Rachael and have the potential to change the course of her life. She had seen that in girls she mentored. A messy breakup often led to disaster in other ways, and if Rachael was as sweet as Josiah said, she would hate to see her go down that path on top of what she had already been through. But from what Josiah said, it sounded like she was going to be all right, and she was glad for Josiah's sake too because he'd been hard on himself for letting it go as long as it had, and writing that letter had been difficult for him.

Her time of worship that evening was very personal and sweet. Kevin was on stage as usual, and she got lost in her thoughts and experience of her faithful and loving Savior. Afterwards while she was waiting for Kevin to finish with putting away the keyboard and helping with the teardown of the room, she sat in a quiet corner and read her Bible.

Last weekend when she and Kevin had spent Saturday afternoon at the park, she had wanted to have her time with God like usual, and they both spent time reading their Bibles individually while sitting at a picnic table together. She read some, wrote in her journal, and did part of a lesson in her devotional book, but Kevin had just sat there reading the entire time.

When she asked him what he was reading, he said, "Psalms. I read them over and over. They make the most sense to me." He explained how his reading comprehension had been limited when he was young and still was a struggle at times. His dad had introduced him to God by reading him Bible stories, and when he was twelve he had started reading the Psalms every night on his own. He had connected with the words and knew what they meant deep within his heart without anyone having to explain it to him.

He still read them every day, and he'd lost count of how many times he had gone all the way through and then started back at the beginning. He knew a lot of them by heart, and he had his favorites, which he shared with her. Since then she had been reading one Psalm a day before she went to sleep, and she was enjoying them also. She always had, but now she saw them through Kevin's eyes, and they had taken on new and deeper meaning.

He caught her in the middle of Psalm 8, the one she had read last night. While she had been sitting here waiting for him, she had started at number one and read through them all again. He sat beside her, and she read verses three, four, and five out loud:

"When I consider your heavens, the work of your fingers, the moon and the stars which you have set in place, what is man that you are

mindful of him, the son of man that you care for him? You made him a little lower than the heavenly beings and crowned him with glory and honor."

He smiled and said the rest from memory in a poetic voice that was different from the way he usually talked. It was beautiful.

"One of your favorites?" she asked.

"Yes."

"What do you think it means: He has crowned us with glory and honor?"

He answered without hesitation. "He is proud to have us as His children who are proudly reigning with Him and calling Him our God."

"I thought pride was a sin."

"Not that kind of pride. It's not prideful to know we are special in God's eyes, because we are. It's wrong to think we know better than God, but not to believe what He tells us."

Kerri smiled. She loved a good spiritual debate and often got into them with her brother and certain friends and classmates. But she couldn't do that with Kevin. God was a black and white issue for him. Theology wasn't complex, it was simple. He left no room for argument.

She had already spent the afternoon with him, and they both had studying to do, so he drove her back to the campus and walked her to the outside door. One of the things his dad had told him when he'd started college was he should never go into a girl's room or into an all-girls' dorm, even if he was invited. He'd told her that when she tried to invite him to walk her upstairs last weekend, and she knew it was better to have him stick with his rules than convince him he could make an exception for her.

He didn't have any qualms about kissing her, however, and she enjoyed his tender affection like always. She knew his dad must have also talked to him about what he could and couldn't do when he was with a girl because with as passionate as his kisses were, he never tried to do anything else or expressed a desire to do so.

She had been debating about bringing up the subject and telling him what had happened to her when she was fourteen. It sometimes came to mind when he kissed her, and the memory made her feel guarded and not fully able to trust him. It wasn't him, it was the person who had hurt her.

With Dylan she had talked to him about it long before he'd ever kissed her and so when he did, it had been a non-issue, but she hadn't had that chance with Kevin, and she thought she could let it go, but she kept imagining him doing something he wouldn't realize was wrong until it was too late, and she didn't want that for him or herself.

Telling him now wasn't the right moment. It needed to be sometime when they had complete privacy and she could talk to him about it, not mention it in the middle of a good-night kiss. She wouldn't be seeing him for a few days, and she decided she would do it then.

"I don't want to say good night," he said, gently running his hand over her back and leaning his forehead against hers.

"When will I see you again?" she asked.

"How about tomorrow?"

She smiled. "We both have to work."

"Tuesday?"

She had to work in the afternoon. Her evening was free, but she would need that time to study. She knew he worked Wednesdays, and Thursday seemed too far away. "Maybe for a little while," she said. "Do you want to have dinner with me?"

"Here?"

"Yes. I work until six."

"I'll be here," he said.

"Where? Right here?"

"Right here. Six o'clock."

"It might be six-ten before I get over here."

"I'll be here at six. I'll wait."

"Okay," she said. "I have something I want to talk to you about."

"What?"

"I'll tell you on Tuesday."

"Tell me now."

"I can't. Tuesday will be better."

"If you tell me now, I can stay longer."

She smiled and wanted to give in, but there wasn't enough privacy here, and they couldn't go for a walk because it was raining. "Tuesday," she said again.

"Okay," he said. "Good night, Kerri."

"Good night."

She stepped away and went inside. Going upstairs, she found all of her roommates studying, so it was easy to get started. She didn't have much to do, just reading and going over her notes. She had done well on her midterms, and it was good to see how different teachers functioned with what types of materials tended to be on the exams. Some had gone strictly from in-class lectures, others from the book, and her psychology class had been a mixture of the two, so she wanted to be more diligent about her reading to be familiar with what the professor didn't cover.

She had finished up with the chapter and gone over the review questions when the phone rang. She reached for it because she was at her desk but Jess was lying on her bed, seeming frustrated with her math at the moment.

"Hello?"

"Hi, is this Kerri?"

"Yes."

"Hi, Kerri. This is Jenna."

Kerri felt alarmed. Kevin should have gotten home by now. Had he not made it? "Hi, Jenna. What's wrong?"

"I'm not sure, actually."

"Is Kevin there?"

"Yeah, he's here, but he's not right. He keeps going to the refrigerator and standing there but not getting anything to eat, and then he goes back to the table and then gets up again two minutes later. I tried to talk to him, but he's not speaking. Did you guys have a fight or something?"

"No," she said, trying to think of anything she had said or done that might have upset him. The only thing that came to mind was her telling him she had something to talk to him about on Tuesday but making him wait. She told Jenna how their evening had ended but didn't share the specific details of what she needed to tell him.

"Yeah, that might be it," she said.

Kerri wasn't sure what to do. She didn't want to tell him over the phone, but she didn't want to leave Kevin in a state of anxiety and confusion. He'd done nothing wrong, but now he was paying for someone else's mistake.

"I'm sure he would drive back up if you don't mind telling him tonight," Jenna said.

"I don't mind, but there's no place here to really talk. I was thinking on Tuesday we could go for a walk if this rain lets up."

"I can try to talk to him," Jenna said. "Now that I know what it is, I might get somewhere. Is it okay for me to say, 'Don't worry about it, it's not anything important', or is that not true?"

"It's important to me, something about my past. I'd probably feel better if I didn't wait. Could I come there?"

"Yeah, absolutely."

"Okay, I'll do that."

She had never been to their apartment, so Jenna gave her directions and it didn't sound too complicated, but it was already nine o'clock so she hoped she didn't get lost. When she told Jess what was going on, Jess offered to go with her, but she had another thought. Seth would be getting off work about now. He was either already here, on his way, or still at Tony's. Sometimes when it was busy on Sunday nights he stayed later.

She decided to call him, and he was at work but about ready to leave. He always rode with Chad on Sundays because she needed the car to get to church. She told him what had happened and asked if he would mind waiting for her to get there so he could go with her. He said that was fine.

"I'm sorry. If I wouldn't have said anything and just waited—"

"You didn't know how he would react," he said. "It's fine. I'll be here."

"Do you have a lot of studying to do?"

"No. I don't put mine off until Sunday night."

"Oh, yeah. I forgot I'm related to Mr. Perfect."

"I'm not perfect, Kerri. Come on, this is what brothers are for."

"Okay, thanks," she said. "Pray for me, okay? I just decided to tell him an hour ago, and I'm not sure I'm ready."

"I will. See you in a few."

"Okay, bye."

She asked Jessica to pray for her too, and then she left, praying for herself all the way into town. She knew she needed to do this, but there was a part of her that really didn't want to. She hadn't had trouble telling others in the past, but she didn't know how much Kevin knew or understood about physical intimacy and why this would be an issue for her.

Seth offered to drive when she arrived at Tony's, and she let him, giving him the directions verbally as they approached the Humboldt Campus area. There were a lot of apartments, but they found the right building, and Seth said he would wait in the car unless she wanted him to come up.

"No, I want to tell him by myself. I'll be all right," she said, realizing if Kevin was the guy she thought he was, she really would be. So far he'd been exactly what she needed.

Seth gave her a hug and told her something he'd told her many times before and yet she still had trouble believing. "It's not your fault, Kerri. What Jeff did to you was wrong, not the other way around. And you have every right to demand better from anyone else."

Chapter Twenty-Three

Kevin was standing in front of the refrigerator, gazing at the food all neatly arranged in their places. He wanted a snack, but he wasn't sure what he wanted, and he didn't want anything enough to move it from its place. He closed the door once again, realizing he'd done so several times now. He'd felt himself turning inward all the way home, and he didn't know how to snap out of it. He couldn't remember why exactly, but something wasn't right.

Jenna met him before he got back to the table. Her presence annoyed him because he'd been set on getting back to his studying, but now she was in the way. She had already bothered him several times, asking if he was okay. Yes, he was fine. Why did she keep asking that? But this time her words were different.

"Kevin, I called Kerri. She's on her way here."

Kerri? Why would she call Kerri? He voiced his thoughts and was surprised at the shakiness of his voice. "I-I j-just s-saw, her. Why-Why is s-she co—"

Jenna interrupted. "Something's wrong Kevin. You're not right. She's coming to talk to you."

"I-I'm a-a—" he took a deep breath and tried again. "I'm all r-right."

"You're not," Jenna said. "She has something to tell you. Do you remember that?"

She has something to tell me. Yes, I remember now. But I don't want to know! It's bad. It's a change. I'm not going to like it!

"D-Don't c-call her."

"I already did. She's coming. Come here and sit with me."

He went with her, but he didn't want to sit down. When it was bad, people always wanted him to sit down. He didn't want to know!

"Sit, Kevin. Sit here with me until she gets here."

"No."

Jenna sat on the couch, but he remained standing. "Kevin, listen to me. If you don't want to sit, that's fine, but I want you to listen, okay? This is important. It's important for Kerri."

He would listen for Kerri.

"She has something she wants to tell you, something about her past. I don't know what it is, but I think she needs you to be here for her right now. All here, you know what I mean? Can you get yourself here?"

She needs me. He felt calmer. He sat down. "Wh-What does she need?"

"I don't know. Just you, I think. Just for you to listen and be who you are."

"W-When? When will she b-be here?"

"In ten minutes."

"What do I say?"

"I don't know. Whatever you're thinking. Just be you and listen."

"A-Are you going to be here?"

"I'll be in my room. If you need me, I'll be here, but I think it's Kerri who really needs someone, and that's you."

He nodded. "Okay."

He got up and roamed the room. Seeing his Bible sitting beside his backpack, he picked it up and turned to Psalm 8. Reading the words reminded him of being with her earlier, and that calmed him. By the time he heard the knock at the door, he felt like he should be anxious and go inside of himself again, but he didn't. Kerri needed him, and he would remain here.

***

Jenna opened the door, and Kerri stepped inside. A feeling of safeness came over her with Jenna's welcoming smile and hug. Jenna seemed happy she had come, and she didn't feel anxious about seeing Kevin like she had on the drive here. There was something about his nearness that always set her at ease.

"How is he?" she whispered.

"Okay. I'll leave you alone, but I'll be in my room if you need me."

"Thanks," she said. Jenna stepped around the corner, and Kerri walked toward the light and saw it was coming from a cozy living room. Kevin was standing there in the middle of it, and she knew she needed one of his hugs before she explained her presence.

He welcomed her easily, and she remained quiet. He spoke first, and his words made her smile. "It's not Tuesday yet, silly."

He was teasing her. That was a good sign. "I know. Jenna said you were upset, so I came."

"She said you need me."

She smiled. "Yes, I do. Can we talk?"

"Sure," he said.

She stepped over to the couch and sat down, but he seemed reluctant to follow her. "Can you sit with me while we talk?"

"Okay."

He came to join her, and she reached for his hand. She had been a mess on the way here, but now she felt safe, and she wanted to set Kevin at ease too.

"This isn't about you, Kevin. I'm not mad at you. You haven't done anything wrong. I'm not unhappy with you or our relationship. Everything's fine. I just need to tell you something about me, and it's hard for me to say, okay?"

"Okay."

"Jenna is right that I need you, and that's why I'm here. I was concerned about you, but now that I see you're okay, I'm just going to tell you this, all right?"

"All right."

She started by telling him about when she was fourteen and had become really boy-crazy with a bunch of different crushes on guys. Some at school, some at church, most of them not really the kind of guys she should have been interested in, including one particular guy in her youth group who was two years older than her. She hung around him and his friends a lot and dressed a certain way to get his attention.

"Our youth group went on a retreat one weekend, and he told me he liked me and asked me out, but my parents wouldn't let me date yet, so he asked me to spend the afternoon with him there, and we went for a walk."

She stopped to make sure Kevin was following her so far. He said he was, and she continued, telling him how at one point after they were pretty far away from the main area, Jeff had kissed her, and she felt like all her dreams were coming true until he started touching her in ways he shouldn't and pulling her against him, and how she couldn't push herself away because he was so strong and holding her so tight.

"When I finally broke free, I just turned and ran, and I don't know what he might have done—how far he would have taken it if I hadn't, and it really shook me up. I became really cautious after that about being around guys. In a way I'm glad it happened because it probably kept me from going too far with other guys who might have been less forceful about it, but it hurt me a lot, and it's still hard for me to-to trust, and—"

Kevin stopped her with a comforting hug, and she started crying. She could still feel Jeff's hands on her and his arms holding her so tight at times. It was a sharp contrast to the safeness she felt with Kevin, and yet she couldn't help but wonder how long that would last. She needed his love and affection. She wanted it. But would it come at too high a price? Did the guy she had been praying for even exist? Could she demand better from Kevin and actually get it?

She cried for a long time, and Kevin was so patient, just holding her and seeming to understand her pain even if he didn't fully understand what she was saying. On the night of the recital when he first kissed her, she asked him if he'd ever kissed a girl before, and he said that he hadn't, so she knew he may not have any frame of reference for what she was saying about Jeff, and yet his comfort was very real and compassionate. And when he did speak, it was exactly what she needed to hear.

"I'll take care of you, Kerri. I won't be like Jeff. I won't do that to you."

"If I told you what Jeff did to me but I didn't tell you it was wrong, would you know that?"

"Yes," he replied. "My dad says, 'Hug girls but not too tight. Don't kiss girls unless they say it's okay. And don't touch—even if they say it's okay.'"

"And you listen to your dad," she stated.

"Yes. He always tells me what I need to know, and I usually listen. When I don't, I get in trouble. So I listen."

"I like all your rules about not being in my dorm and not kissing me in the car and stuff like that."

"Can I still kiss you, or do you need me to stop?"

"I love your kisses. You don't have to stop."

"Can I kiss you right now?"

She knew kissing here was a habit she didn't want to start. "How about if you walk me outside first?"

"Okay."

She smiled and got up to leave. Before they went out, she stepped into the hallway and knocked on Jenna's door. Jenna invited her in.

"Thanks for calling me."

"Thanks for coming. Is everything okay?"

"Yes. Kevin's a good listener."

"With a pure heart," Jenna added. "Whatever he said, you can believe him."

"I do," she said. "He's going to walk me out. Good night."

"Good night, Kerri."

She turned to leave, but Jenna stopped her.

"And Kerri?"

"Yeah?"

"I want you to know I'm here if you ever need to talk. About Kevin or your relationship or whatever. Anything. Honestly."

"Thanks, Jenna," she said, stepping back to give her a hug. "I feel like I'm beginning the greatest adventure of my life and I have no idea where I'm going."

"Straight to my brother's heart, I'd say. It's a narrow gate, but somehow you managed to find it."

Jenna's words remained with her as she stepped outside with Kevin and he walked her down to the lower level. Once they were on the sidewalk, she turned to face him and took both of his hands. There was something specific she had been looking for in the guys she chose to date, and she hadn't thought about it with Kevin until now, but she knew it had been true all along. So true she didn't have to think twice about it once Jenna's words had reminded her.

She had been looking for someone who showed her Jesus, and she knew that could only come from a pure heart like Kevin had. It hadn't been easy to find. She'd searched and waited and searched some more, and although she knew Kevin wasn't the only one, she knew he was the only one who connected with her heart as easily as she had connected with his.

"You have a pure heart, Kevin," she said. "Do you know that?"

"What's that mean?"

"It means you're genuine, authentic, completely transparent."

"Is that good?"

She smiled. "It's very good. It means I see God in you."

"How?"

"In your love for me, in your joy, in your kindness, in the way you protect me. No one's had to teach you that, it's just there because God is. You don't just say you know Him, you actually do. You know Him on a heart-level."

"Doesn't everyone?"

"No. I haven't always, and I still struggle with it sometimes—bringing God from someplace out there to right here in my life, knowing without a doubt He's with me and everything I need."

Kevin appeared confused.

"You have it, Kevin. It's just a part of who you are, the way God has wired your mind and heart. You read Psalms, and you get it. Someone tells you, 'This is right and this is wrong,' and you believe it without having to learn the hard way. Most of us aren't that smart."

"You think I'm smart?"

"I think you're the smartest guy I've ever met."

She mirrored his warm smile and gave him a sweet kiss. She knew Seth could see them from where he was parked, but she didn't care if he saw them kissing. Seth often said, 'If you don't have anything to hide, then why hide it?' And she liked that philosophy.

"Can I still come up on Tuesday?" Kevin asked before she stepped away.

"Yes."

"Okay. I'll be there."

She returned to the car where Seth was patiently waiting. He didn't ask for any details until they were back on the road. She told him everything, and he seemed satisfied that she was satisfied.

"I see Jesus in him, Seth. Do you think he sees Jesus in me?"

"Yes."

"How do you know?"

"Because I do. It's pretty hard to miss."

"How so?"

"A lot of ways, but I think the way Kevin sees it most is in your ability to reach his heart. Not everyone can do that, very few, in fact. And I think that has to be from God."

Kerri had a sense of peace come over her for another reason too. Something she had been considering even before she'd met Kevin was to pursue a career in helping those with special needs. Lately she had been thinking a lot about becoming a special education teacher, and Seth's words confirmed God may have gifted her in that particular way. Maybe she could only reach Kevin's heart because she was specifically meant to do so, or maybe she could reach others like him too.

She decided for now, that's what she would set her sights on. She would continue to wait for God's leading and confirmation, but the joy in her heart told her she had to be doing something right.

Chapter 5

Josiah felt nervous about calling Rachael, but he knew he should, and he knew he wanted to. After calling him two weeks ago, she had called him last Sunday afternoon also. He thought she might again today, but he didn't want her to have to be the initiator again. It was his turn to let her know he really did want to be a friend to her, and he wanted to keep his hopes alive it could become more than that in the future.

He wasn't sure if it was appropriate for him to be feeling that way about her, or if she had any interest in him whatsoever, but even if he could just brighten her day a little and remind her life would go on, that was enough for him. He'd liked other girls before but had never felt any genuine concern for them. He hadn't gotten to know them well enough, but he was getting to know Rachael. They had talked for an hour last Sunday, and she had written him a letter he received in the mail yesterday.

When Rachael answered the phone, she didn't sound surprised to be hearing from him. "Hi, Josiah," she said. "How are you?"

"I'm fine. How are you?"

is is a nice surprise."

it was my turn.   I got your letter

ood.   I hope it wasn't too boring."

, not at all.   I liked hearing about your week."

"How was yours?"

"Mostly good," he said.

"Tell me about it.   All the boring details like I did."

He shared what he could remember, and it hadn't been too eventful.   Mostly going to class and studying.

"Do you have a girlfriend?" she asked.   "I don't think I ever asked you that."

"No, I don't."

"I figured you didn't, or you probably would have mentioned her."   She changed the subject.   "Have you heard from Gabe?"

"No, and I haven't tried to reach him.   I'll probably try on Thanksgiving Weekend when he's home and can't use being away at school as an excuse to not be talking to Sienna."

She didn't say anything, and this time he changed the subject.   "How have your times with Jesus been going?"

"Good," she said.   "I need it every day, and I'm glad you encouraged me to do that.   One day this week I was really not doing well, and the house was empty when I came home from school—that's when I usually do it because it helps me to unwind from the day—and I ended up spending like two hours just reading and praying and writing stuff in my journal.   It totally changed my day and the rest of the week."

"That didn't happen to be Thursday, did it?"

"Yes, I think it was.   Why?"

"You were on my mind a lot, and I prayed for you several times."

She was quiet for a moment and then said, "You're making a big difference in my life right now, Josiah. I hope you know that."

He almost said, 'It's the least I can do,' but she didn't want him blaming himself for anything, so he let it go and felt happy he could be making a difference now.

He talked to her until it was time for him to leave for church, and then he wrote her a letter that week along with a couple of online messages where he shared what he had gotten out of his "Time with Jesus" that day. He had started calling it that because that's how Seth always referred to his personal devotion time, and it had made a difference in the way he approached his own.

He wasn't just reading the Bible and praying to some distant, far-away God. He was meeting with Jesus right there in his dorm room, or at the library, or by the lake, and instead of trying to read the Bible and figure it out on his own like he'd done in the past, he often started by asking, 'What do You want to teach me today, Jesus?'

Rachael seemed to appreciate his messages, and she wrote a few in return about how she was seeing God in new ways too. She called him the following Sunday, and they talked for about the same amount of time, and then she asked him what he was doing for Thanksgiving.

"Seth's family is coming on Wednesday and taking him and Amber and Kerri down to San Jose where his grandparents live, and Seth invited me to go too since both Chad and Adam are going home for the weekend."

"Are you missing your family a lot?"

"Some. But being here is good for me right now."

"When does the semester end for you?"

"We have two more weeks of classes after Thanksgiving and then finals."

"Yeah, me too," she said.

He felt nervous about what he wanted to say, but he said it anyway. "I'm taking two days to drive home for Winter Break instead of doing it all in one shot. Seth said I could stay at his house in Portland, and I was thinking that would give me time to stop by and see you on my way up, if you want."

Her response came easily. "I'd love that."

"Okay, I'll let you know what time, but it should be Friday of that week."

"Whenever should be fine," she said. "I'll be here."

***

Flying into Portland on the day before Thanksgiving, Chad felt a mixture of emotions. He was glad he had decided to come home for the holiday weekend with Jessica, even if he had protested her invitation at first. It wasn't that he didn't want to go home or spend the weekend with her, just that she wanted to fly rather than drive, and her family had offered to pay for his plane ticket too since he couldn't afford it.

Her argument had been that she was the one who wanted to fly because she wasn't a great long-distance traveler and it would give her more time with her family, and his argument had been her family shouldn't have to pay for him too just because he didn't have the money. She'd won, but he still felt uneasy about it.

At school their families' different financial status didn't mean much, and he had mostly put it out of his mind until this had come up. Their racial difference had been mostly a non-issue too. Lifegate was more ethnically diverse than he'd expected. Occasionally Chad felt like others on campus or in town gave them a disapproving look, but nothing major. And this weekend he wasn't concerned about being treated any differently by her family than in August, but he was a little concerned about his own family meeting Jessica. He knew his mom was fine with it, but his stepdad worried him. He could be as prejudiced toward white people as some whites were toward blacks.

But no matter their differences, he had fallen in love with her during the past three months. He didn't know if the feeling was mutual. He hadn't told her that, and she didn't seem overly anxious to hear it, at least she had never said anything. From his perspective they had the perfect relationship, and he was very happy. But he didn't know if she felt that way or not. He didn't think she was unhappy, but perhaps she was looking for something more than he had to give.

She had fallen asleep on his shoulder twenty minutes ago, and he hated to wake her, but he knew he would be in a few minutes anyway. Taking her hand and bringing her fingers to his lips, he kissed her skin softly until she stirred. Slowly opening her eyes and giving him a gentle smile, she asked if they were about to land.

"Yes. I thought us landing might startle you if you were asleep."

"Thanks, you're probably right."

After they landed, he followed her into the terminal. When they reached the area where small shops and food places were located, he asked if she wanted to stop and get something to drink or if she was hungry. Her dad wasn't picking them up for another half-hour because he was stopping by on his way home from work.

"I'm starving!" she laughed. "I think those airplane pretzels just make me more hungry."

He bought her a slice of pizza and one for himself, and they got a Coke to share. Sitting at one of the tables to eat and talking until it was close to the time her dad said he would meet them, they walked the rest of the way through the terminal and went outside to wait on the sidewalk for him to drive up.

"It's cold here," she said, zipping up her jacket and snuggling close to him for warmth.

He laughed. "Are you turning into a California girl already?"

"I guess so," she said.

When her dad didn't arrive immediately, he decided to ask her something he had wanted to ask her on the plane, but it had been a crowded flight and too noisy.

"Are you happy, sweetheart?"

She looked up and stared at him curiously. "What do you mean?"

"Happy with me? Happy with us?"

"Yes."

He wondered if that was a real answer or only what she knew he wanted to hear. He couldn't bring himself to question her, but she saw the doubt in his face.

Kissing him tenderly, she convinced him a little more with her touch and her words. "I am, Chad. I'm very happy."

He had to say it even though a huge part of him feared her reaction. "Me too. I'm in love with you, Jessica."

She gave him a gentle smile and appeared close to tears, but she didn't say the words in return.

"Is that okay?" he asked.

"Yes."

They were both silent for a moment and then she spoke again. "I don't know if I'm ready to say that to you yet. Is that okay?"

"Do you think you ever will, or am I not the guy you're looking for?"

"I think you're a definite possibility."

"What more do I need to do? What do you need from me?"

"Just time," she said.

"More time with me?" he asked, not knowing if he could give her that with their busy schedules. He was already giving her everything he had to give.

"No, you give me plenty of time, Chad. I mean more time for our relationship to grow, and more time for my heart to heal."

Hearing that made his heart rest a little easier. Kissing her this time, he allowed himself to show her a deeper form of affection than usual. He was completely in love with her, but he hadn't let her know that yet—with his words or the way he kissed her.

"Does this mean you're not mad at me anymore?"

"I wasn't mad," he said. "I've never been mad at you. I'm just scared."

"Scared of what?"

"Not being who you need me to be. My dad—"

"Your dad what?"

"He was unemployed most of the time he and my mom were married, and she always supported him instead of the other way around."

"You're not your dad."

"You paid for my ticket today."

"My parents paid," she said. "I'm not even working right now. I don't know how you do it and still get all your studying done."

He was doing well in all of his classes and didn't feel like college was as tough as he thought it might be. And he liked working at Tony's. He did deliveries mostly and got paid well enough in tips each night to have extra spending-money to treat Jessie like he wanted to.

"You're smart, Chad, and you work hard, and if you didn't spend so much of your money on me with all the dates and little gifts, you would've had the money for your own ticket. It was my fault for not telling you sooner."

Her dad drove up at that moment, and he got out to give Jessie a hug.

"Hello, Chad," Mr. Shaw said, shaking his hand. "How are you?"

"I'm very well," he said. Jessie was still in her dad's arms. "Your daughter takes good care of me."

Jessica smiled and said something he would always be honored to hear, but especially right in front of her dad.

"You're the one who takes good care of me, Chad Michael Williams."

He held her gaze and knew he was making a vow to her with Mr. Shaw there to hear his words. Words he meant with all of his heart.

"And I will for as long as you'll let me."

Chapter Twenty-Five

Jessica hadn't expected coming home with Chad to feel like this. She had been enjoying their relationship very much, and she knew she wanted it to continue. She knew her family would be welcoming of him, and she had talked to her mom over the phone about their relationship enough for her parents to know Chad may be a part of her life for a long time.

Her mom had once asked her if she thought she could marry him, and she said yes. She knew she could marry him someday, but she wasn't in any rush for that to happen. She needed time to heal from her past hurts and mistakes, and she also needed time to know for sure if Chad was the one she was meant to spend the rest of her life with.

But standing here now, having him say a serious and caring thing right in front of her dad, on top of what he had already told her a few minutes ago, she suddenly felt different than she had for the past three months. Chad wasn't just a nice guy she was dating. They fit together. Having him here felt right and comfortable. And she had the most amazing feeling sweep through her.

I am in love with him!

She simply smiled at him for now, wondering if she was feeling overly emotional or if something genuine was happening in her heart. But as the evening progressed, she knew it was more than a fleeting thought. Dinner with her family was relaxing and filled with conversation and laughter. Chad seemed completely at ease, even though this was the first time he had spent a significant amount of time with them, and she felt comfortable with him there.

Because Chad was going to be having Thanksgiving Dinner with her family tomorrow and they were eating around one o'clock, they had already decided he would spend the night here and they would go to see his family later in the afternoon tomorrow. After her parents and brother had gone upstairs, she wanted more time with him, and they decided to watch a movie.

While they were waiting for the menu screen to appear, he pulled her close to him and spoke gently. "I hope I didn't say too much earlier."

"About what?"

"When I said that about wanting to take care of you for as long as you'll let me. If that made you uncomfortable—"

"No. Not at all," she interrupted, almost laughing he sounded so worried about it. "I really liked hearing that."

"Right in front of your dad?"

"Especially in front of my dad!" She laughed. "When you told me you were in love with me, I thought, 'That's nice. I can handle that.' But when you spoke those words, I knew you were really serious."

"I am, Jessica."

"I know you are, and I'm glad. I'm not sure I realized it until tonight, or maybe I wasn't sure you felt the same way, but I am completely in love with you, Chad. I'm sorry I couldn't say it earlier, but I've spent the last five hours thinking it."

"Are you sure? You don't have to say it just because—"

"I'm sure. I know what I've been waiting for, and it's you. I've just been a little scared to believe it can last and be as good as I think it is."

He smiled and kissed her. "Me too. We'll believe it together, okay?"

"Okay."

***

Kerri enjoyed the familiar surroundings of her grandparents' California home. She had been coming here twice a year for as long as she could remember. Seeing her parents again, after being away at college for three months, along with her older siblings was good too. She had missed them all. Being with them on Thanksgiving Day was as good as it had always been, and having the break from school was definitely needed, and yet by Friday evening she was really missing Kevin.

Normally she worked at The Oasis on Friday nights, and that kept her busy until she could see him on Saturday morning, but tonight she felt restless. Seeing Josiah take his phone and go onto the deck to call someone, she decided to do the same and went upstairs to the room she was sharing with Amber. She

265

called the restaurant, instead of Kevin's phone, because she didn't want to interrupt him if he was busy, and Tony answered.

"Is he super-busy right now, or could I talk to him for a minute?"

"You can have more than a minute," he said. "I'll tell him to take his break now and have him call you back."

"Okay, thanks."

She hung up and waited for her phone to ring, and it did a minute later. "That was fast," she said. "You must not have been in the middle of a pizza."

"No," he said. "It's slow tonight."

"What else did you do today?"

"I studied this morning and then went to the park."

She gave him the run-down of her day which consisted of shopping with Amber, her sister, her mom, and a few others, and then going to see a movie this afternoon with Seth, Amber, and Josiah. Not having much more to talk about, she decided to tell him something she had been thinking. They were going to be signing up for their classes for Spring Semester next week, and she had brought the catalog with her and made her final decisions after dinner.

She hadn't said anything to Kevin about her possible interest in going into Special Education, so she told him that along with the two classes she was going to select to get her started in that direction: *Introduction To Teaching*, and *Child Development*.

"I know," he said.

"What do you mean, you know? I haven't told you that."

"I just know. I'm a smart guy, you know."

She wasn't sure if he was teasing her, or if he really did have some kind of premonition of what she had been thinking about, but she went with it.

"Yes, I know. You've got me all figured out."

"Pretty much."

"And you know how much I'm missing you right now, and how I have no idea how I'm going to make it over Winter Break?"

In another three weeks she was going to be heading home, and the following Monday he would be leaving for New York for two weeks. He had an aunt and uncle who lived there, and they had been the ones who had gotten Kevin interested in traveling. He usually went there in the summer to visit them, and he'd gone to Europe with them this year and to Australia a couple of years ago. He had always wanted to go to New York City around Christmas when he could see the big tree in Rockefeller Center and go ice skating, so they'd invited him to spend Christmas with them this year.

"You could come with me," he said.

He had told her that several times now. "I'd love to, but I don't think my parents would go for that."

"Have you talked to them about Alaska yet?"

Next summer he was going to Alaska, and she did think that would be a cool place to visit, but she didn't think her parents would let her go off to Alaska for the summer with her boyfriend any more than they would let her go to New York for Christmas.

"Maybe someday I'll go on a trip with you," she said, thinking of a specific time in her mind, but she didn't know if Kevin would catch on to what she was saying.

"And where exactly do you want to go for our honeymoon?" he said.

She smiled. He was much more perceptive than people often gave him credit for, including her.

"I won't say no then."

"I know you won't," he said.

***

Rachael liked this spontaneous side of Josiah. She had expected him to maybe call her on Sunday since it was his turn again, but having him call on Friday night was very surprising. She had been enjoying their phone conversations and especially the messages he had been sending her over the last couple of weeks. They always made her day.

She asked him what he had been doing since arriving in San Jose on Wednesday, and he sounded glad he had gone with his roommate instead of staying on campus over the extended weekend. She'd had a pretty good day yesterday, but today had been tougher. Last year Gabe had come to visit her on Thanksgiving, and she thought she was going to be spending the holiday with him for many years to come, if not the rest of her life. It still seemed unreal their relationship had unraveled in the first place, let alone in such a complicated way.

Josiah reminded her of Gabe a little bit—in the good ways, like how he made God a priority in his life and the way he made her feel like she was special to him. But he was also very different, and she couldn't tell if Josiah simply saw her as a friend, or if he would like her to be more than that. Gabe had always been obvious about it, but Josiah was a mystery to her.

Either way, he was incredibly sweet and genuine, and he had become her lifeline in all of this right along with Jesus. She had never felt a strong sense of someone outside of her family being a vessel of God's love to her, but she felt that with Josiah.

"Are you still planning to stop by in a few weeks?" she asked. "I'm looking forward to it."

"Yes. And I should be there by late afternoon."

"My mom and dad would be fine with it if you want to spend the night here. If you'd rather stay with Seth, that's fine, but the invitation's open."

"Okay. I might do that depending on when we leave. I'd like more than a quick hello."

"Me too," she said. "It will be good to talk to you face to face. I feel like I miss a lot with you over the phone."

"I'm not a great phone person. I feel like I miss a lot with you too."

"One thing I don't miss is your genuine concern for me. I'm not sure Gabe ever had that. We had a lot of fun together, and he knew how to make me feel good, but I'm not sure he ever really saw me."

"He was a fool, Rachael."

"Maybe I expected too much from a high-school romance."

"Don't lower your expectations just because Gabe didn't meet them. The right guy will. Just like my roommate did for his fiancée."

"Just like you will, Josiah, for the right girl for you. She will be so blessed to have you."

"I hope so," he said.

"I know so. You couldn't let me down without feeling bad, and I'm not even your girlfriend."

He was quiet for a moment, and her heart started beating faster at the thought of him saying, 'I want you to be,' but he said something else.

"Looking back, what's one thing Gabe didn't give you that you really needed, besides the obvious."

She thought seriously about that. Going back to the early stages of their relationship and up until the point when things went sour, she knew of one thing, at least partially. "He gave me his body and his mind—he was very affectionate, and we could talk for hours. But he didn't give me his heart. I think he loved the idea of me, but not me. Not deep down. Not to the point of wanting what I wanted and being the center of his world. That might sound selfish, but that's the way I felt about him."

She started to cry, and it was the first time she had ever done that over the phone with Josiah. They had talked a lot, and she'd always been honest with him, but that was as real as the pain got for her. The absolute core of it all. She had loved Gabe, but he hadn't loved her in return.

Josiah let her cry for a minute, and when he spoke, his words were simple and sincere, and she knew he meant them. "I'm sorry, Rachael. I'm sorry he didn't love you like that."

"I know you are," she whispered.

"But someone will. I knew you were in love with Gabe. I saw it, and it was beautiful. And the guy who is worthy of that love from you will return it."

Chapter Twenty-Six

Kevin knew he should stop playing pinball and go back to work, but he didn't want to. He had spent the whole day with Kerri and enjoyed every moment. They had come back here to make pizza together from four until after the dinner-rush, and then after having dinner themselves, she had left to go back to her campus and pack for her trip home tomorrow. The final weeks of the semester had gone by so fast, and they were both finished with their final exams. He'd been excited about going to New York City to visit his aunt and uncle during the Christmas season, but now he didn't want to go without Kerri. The thought of not seeing her for another eighteen days paralyzed him. Turning inward and shutting out the world was his only defense against the pain.

"Hey, Kev. You coming back?"

He could hear his dad's voice, but he couldn't respond. His complete focus was on the ball right now, and nothing else was getting in.

"I told you to take the rest of the evening off. It's fine if you still want to. We can handle it here."

He saved the ball, but barely. His dad was breaking his concentration. He kept playing, feeling his body getting more tense.

"Is this more about Kerri leaving, or about her not going to New York with you?"

"I want her to go."

"Did you tell her that again tonight?"

"Yes."

"It's a big step for her, Kev. We've talked about this."

He lost the ball and let his anger surface, but he hurt his hand more than the machine. His dad pulled him away from the game and steered him outside. He wanted to hit the side of the building but knew that would hurt too much.

Slumping to the ground instead, he let the tears come. He thought he could change her mind. He had talked her into letting him fly to Portland on New Year's Day, why didn't she want to spend the next two weeks with him too? He had the money for her to go. How could she have driven away like that? It hurt so bad, and he had no idea how to make it stop.

***

Kerri stopped at the grocery store in town to pick up a few things for the trip home tomorrow. Making her selections, she tried to put the image of Kevin's tears and sad eyes out of her mind, but it wasn't easy. Turning away from his pleading, painful expression had been very difficult.

But it was ridiculous for her to go to New York with him. He would be all right once he was there. He'd just been upset tonight because he was going to miss her, but they couldn't always avoid that. If it didn't happen now, it would at another time. Her parents wouldn't want her missing Christmas, let alone flying across the country with a guy they barely knew.

Going back to her car, feeling determined to not give it another thought, she started the engine and heard the music begin to play. It was in the middle of a song, one of her favorites, so she pushed the button to have it go back to the beginning. Once she had pulled onto the highway, she sang along with the familiar words of the chorus:

It's not about my plans
It's not about my ways
It's not about anything
Except for this

It's all about His plans for me
And what He has to show me
And the blessings He's ready to
Pour out on me

If I just believe
If I just listen
If I just believe when He says
Just trust in Me

God interrupted her singing. *Are you trusting me in this, Kerri?*

In what?

In your relationship with Kevin.

Yes! That's all I've been doing for the past two months.

And now? About New York?

Yes—maybe.

Kevin's sad eyes returned to her thoughts along with the conversations they'd had about her going to New York with him. He hadn't been demanding about it, just persistent, and she thought it was sweet.

But tonight had been different. "Please, Kerri?" he said with tears in his eyes. "I really want you to go."

"I'm sorry, Kevin. I can't," she said, giving him a hug and letting him hold her for a long time.

He hadn't said anything, not even good-bye when she kissed him and left him standing there by the car.

The song reached the chorus once again, and this time she just listened.

It's not about my plans
It's not about my ways
It's not about anything
Except for this

It's all about His plans for me
And what He has to show me
And the blessings He's ready to
Pour out on me

If I just believe
If I just listen
If I just believe when He says
Just trust in Me

"Okay, God. I'm listening," she said, approaching the intersection where she would make the turn to head back to the campus. "What am I supposed to do?"

Call your mom and dad.

Now?

Now.

She pulled into the gas station on the corner and parked in one of the parking spaces in front of the mini mart, but she had no plans to go inside and grab a candy bar. Taking her phone out of her purse, she placed the call home, and her dad answered.

"Hi, Daddy. It's Kerri."

"Hey, sweetheart. You all right?"

"Yes. I just have something to ask you."

"Okay."

"What would you and mom think of me going to New York with Kevin? He's been asking me, and I've been telling him you would never let me, but I never actually asked you. It's okay to say no. I'm just wondering."

"Do you want to?"

She gave him an honest answer. "Yeah, maybe. I've been thinking I'm not ready for that, but I don't know why. His sister is going, and I get along fine with her. Kevin takes care of me in everything else, I know he would do the same there. I'd love to go, but I'd miss Christmas, and I understand if you and mom want me there instead."

"I think this is something you have to decide for yourself, sweetheart. We would love to have you here, but you need to do what's right for you."

An excited feeling entered her heart at the thought of actually going. She had been saying, 'I'd love to, but I can't.' But she could! She could imagine the look on Kevin's face when she told him, and that brought a very warm feeling to her heart.

"I think I want to," she said. "We would be back on New Year's, and I'd still have two weeks at home. School doesn't start until the 21st."

"They'll be other Christmases, sweetheart. And Christmas isn't about one day; it's about our whole lives and what we do all year round to experience God's best for us."

She'd heard her dad say that before, and she knew this was all about trusting God and allowing Him to teach her things and bless her through a new experience. She had been thinking of it in a logical way, but God's ways didn't always follow logic, and neither did Kevin's.

"Can I talk to Mom?"

"Sure. I love you, sweetheart."

"I love you too, Daddy."

Her mom came on the line, and she told her the same things she had told her dad, and her mom's response was similar, which she expected since her parents were usually on the same page about things.

"Thanks, Mom. I don't know why I waited so long to ask."

"It's a whole new world, isn't it?"

"Being in love, you mean?"

"Yes."

She laughed. "Yes, but I'm loving it. I can't wait to tell him!"

"Then I'd better let you go. Do you need us to send you some money?"

"No, I have enough. Kevin's paying for my ticket and everything. I'll call you this weekend and give you all the details."

"Okay. I love you, baby."

"Love you too, Mom. Bye."

Lowering the phone from her ear, she turned it off and sighed. "Are you sure, God? Is that the right decision?"

Yes.

Driving back to the restaurant, she pulled into an open space by the door, and she went inside. Tony wasn't at the counter, and stepping into the kitchen, she saw no sign of Kevin either.

"Hi, Kerri," Blake said. "I thought you left."

"I did. Did Kevin leave too?"

"I don't think so. He was playing pinball the last I saw."

She smiled at him, unable to contain the news. "I changed my mind."

"About New York?"

"Yes," she laughed.

"I'm sure he'll be very happy to hear that."

She went into the dining area and headed for the pinball machines and video games, but she didn't see him there either. Catching sight of Tony on the sidewalk outside the door, she stepped out.

"Where's Kevin?"

He pointed to the ground on the other side of the door. Kevin had his head in his hands and his knees tucked into his chest. She would have felt completely awful if she didn't know she would be speaking the words he wanted to hear. He'd been very settled these last two months, and she had almost forgotten how he could get sometimes. He had been a little upset about her leaving at Thanksgiving, but just sad, not like this.

"It's okay," she whispered to Tony. "I'll take it from here."

He smiled and went inside without hesitation. His family's confidence in her to be exactly what Kevin needed at any given moment amazed her, as did her ability to do so, but she had it. There was no denying that.

She sat beside him, stroking his hair and saying his name. He looked up, but there was a hollow expression on his face, like he wasn't sure where he was or if it was really her.

"It's me. I came back. I have something to tell you."

"Kerri," he whispered.

She kissed him gently. "It's all right," she said. "I changed my mind. I want to go with you."

"You do?"

"Yes. Is that all right?"

"Yes. I really want you to go."

"Yeah, I got that," she laughed. "I love you, Kevin. I want to go. Thank you for asking me."

His body relaxed, and she moved herself onto his lap, allowing him to hold her close for several minutes. He didn't say anything, and neither did she. And something she had known in the back of her mind all along became an absolute reality for her during those moments.

She was going to marry Kevin someday, and he was such a gift. A gift sent straight from Heaven: a perfect gift she had asked and waited for. And there was nothing to fear. Nothing to be cautious about. Neither God nor Kevin was giving her that option. All she could do was embrace the blessings and believe in the faithfulness of her God.

No, this wasn't about her plans and ways. It was about the amazing plans God had for her. Just living in the reality of His love and trusting Him every step of the way.

Chapter Twenty-Seven

Kerri stayed outside with Kevin until he became his normal self, but she needed to get back to the campus and tell Seth her new plans before he went to bed. Kevin let her go without tears this time, but he did hold her longer than usual beside the car, thanking her for changing her mind and promising to take care of her in New York.

"I know you will, Kevin. I never doubted that."

"Can I see you tomorrow?"

"Yes. Do you have to work?"

"Not until four. Lauren and Adam are taking the early shift."

"I'll come down with them and meet you here."

He kissed her, and it was a much better kiss than he had given her an hour ago. "I love you, Kerri," he said, holding her cheek in his hand and staring straight into her soul. "I'm so glad you're coming."

"Me too."

"Good night."

"Good night, Kevin. I love you too," she said, taking his hand from her face and kissing his fingers. "I'll see you tomorrow."

Heading back to the campus, she decided to go to Seth's room and see if he was there. She imagined he would be, since he needed to pack for their trip tomorrow and Amber would need to be doing the same. He was, and he appeared concerned when he opened the door and saw her standing there.

"Can I talk to you?"

"Sure," he said, stepping into the hallway. There was a small lounge at the end of his hall, and they walked down to see if it was in use by anyone. It wasn't and they went inside. He closed the door behind her. "What's up?"

"I've decided to go to New York with Kevin. I called Mom and Dad, and they're fine with it. I told Kevin I couldn't go for the millionth time, but he cried when I left, and then I realized I hadn't prayed about it, and as soon as I did I knew what I was supposed to do."

"Did you tell him?"

"Yes, I went back, and I'm really glad because he was a mess."

"Are you just going for him or because you want to?"

She smiled. "I want to. I was scared of it and tried to tell myself it was ridiculous for me to go, but it's not. Not with Kevin. He doesn't ask anybody to go on these trips with him."

"And Mom and Dad are okay with it?" he asked.

"Yes," she laughed, stepping forward to give him a hug.

He held her and sighed. "Oh, Kerri. When did we grow up?"

"We? You've been doing this for two years, and you're getting married. I'm just getting started."

He released her and asked a serious question. "And how is it going? You don't talk about it much."

"There's nothing to talk about. I'm completely happy with Kevin and everything about our relationship. We don't fight. He doesn't leave me feeling confused or wondering what he's thinking. Our time together is always good. I think I feel the same way about him as you do about Amber."

"What do you like best about him?"

"He's real with me—always. And I never have to wonder about that."

"And you're real with him?"

"I have to be. And I want to be. Trying to hide anything from Kevin is like trying to hide an elephant in a tiny room. He notices everything."

"Feel like sharing?" he asked, stepping away from her and taking a seat on the nearest sofa. "I really don't see the two of you together much."

She sat beside him and thought for a moment. How did she go about describing the way she felt with Kevin?

"You know how he is about making pizza—how he focuses his complete attention on what he's doing, even if he's made the same pizza a thousand times before?"

"Yes."

"And you know how he is when he talks about someplace he's been—sharing every little detail and finding joy in the most ordinary things?"

"Yes," Seth replied.

"Well, he's that way about me. I'll be thinking something that makes my face change in expression, and I might not even realize I'm thinking about it before he says, 'What are you thinking about?' And when I know I have something to say and am fully prepared to do so, he gets this look of complete concern like I'm going to tell him the sky is falling." She laughed. "I think I prayed one too many times for a guy who would be a good listener and take me seriously."

"I don't think that has anything to do with his autism, sis. He might be more obvious about it, but all guys feel that way about the girl they never want to let go."

She thought for a moment and then asked him something she had wondered often. "How do you think he knew?"

"Knew what?"

"That I was the one he wanted."

"Maybe an angel whispered in his ear."

She smiled. Somehow she didn't doubt it could have been supernatural intervention. "I'm definitely on the receiving end of a gift straight from Heaven."

"And you're a gift to him too, Kerri. I'm sure no one knows that more than he does."

She smiled and gave him another hug. "I hope I can take care of him as well as he takes care of me."

"I'm sure you will," he said. "I'm assuming this means you're not going with us tomorrow?"

"We're leaving on Monday, but I'll be home on New Year's Day."

"And Kevin's coming with you?"

"He'd better be. If I'm going with him to New York, he better be ready to meet the rest of my family and have some crazy days with us."

***

Amber felt really excited about going home. Packing one of her bags for her month-long break, she felt like she'd had a good semester and knew she would miss Seth when she wasn't seeing him every day, but she was ready to be at home for a few weeks, have time with her family, see the friends she had left behind, and she was especially excited about Hope and Ben's wedding taking place this Saturday.

It was kind of a bummer because she would only have half a day with them before they left for their honeymoon, but she was really happy for them. Her excitement hadn't faded when they left early the next morning, and unlike their trip down to California four months ago, their return trip went smoothly. She also felt excited for Kerri and her sudden change of plans to go to New York with Kevin. Seth wasn't surprised and neither was she. Driving back without her seemed perfectly natural. She was glad Lauren was going to be staying at the campus for a few extra days too, so she wouldn't be all alone there, and she was also happy to have the time with Seth all to herself. She would never complain about that.

Seth had originally planned on taking her home tonight and then going back to his house to be there when Josiah came to spend the night. But since Josiah had decided to spend the night at Rachael's house, Seth drove them to the church where they arrived in time for the wedding rehearsal, and he planned to stay tonight and probably until Sunday evening.

She was travel weary, but it was good to see everyone, especially her mom and dad whom she clung to for several moments, and her dad said something to Seth that made tears sting her eyes.

"Thanks for taking good care of her. She looks more radiant than ever."

"I think so," Seth said, pulling her close to him. "Imagine what she'll look like when it's our turn to do this."

Amber smiled at them both and then spotted Hope on the other side of the room. She dashed toward her and gave her a hug also. Hope clung to her and said similar words.

"You look great. I think California has been good to you."

"I like it. And a special person has been there too."

Seth came up behind her.

"You mean this guy?"

"That's him," Amber said. "Where's my brother? He's still the one you're marrying tomorrow, right?"

"Yes, he's around here somewhere. I gave him a couple of errands to run, and he got back about five minutes ago. He's probably either in the kitchen or the youth room."

Amber needed to use the bathroom and was on her way there when she heard Ben behind her.

"Yo, Amber!"

She turned and saw her brother, who made tears come to her eyes instantly. He looked fantastically happy, and she was so happy for him. They had grown up in this church together, run through the hallways as little kids, worshipped God and learned about Him within these walls countless times. And now Ben was getting married. It seemed unreal.

"You look good, sis," he said. "I guess I don't need to ask if Seth's been treating you right."

"But you will anyway."

"That's what big brothers are for."

She smiled. "He's been treating me just fine. Better than fine. He amazes me."

"With an amazing girl like you, what do you expect?"

"What do I expect? You're the one asking!"

He gave her another hug, but he didn't apologize for his protective nature. "I know you know this, but I can't even describe how I feel right now knowing that Hope and I have waited. I used to say this out of principle, but now I can say it out of experience. You won't regret waiting."

"Waiting for what?" Seth said, coming up beside her and whispering in her ear.

She laughed and fell into his arms. Seth greeted Ben over the top of her head. "There's the man," he said. "How does it feel to be less than a day away from marriage?"

"Pretty great," Ben said, shaking his hand and pulling him into a hug like they usually exchanged. "Have you two set a date yet?"

"I think so," Seth said. "We need to check with everyone's May schedules."

"May, huh? That's not too far away."

"No, we decided the sooner the better." Seth laughed at his choice of words. "That didn't come out right. What I mean is, we'd like to get back to our church down there for the summer children's program that begins in June and then come back up here for a couple of weeks in August to relax and visit everyone before Fall Semester begins."

She and Seth had been discussing the timing of their wedding the last few days, but Seth saying it out loud to someone else made it a little more real for her. She smiled at him and felt very much at peace about their current plans. She wasn't going to get her heart totally set on May until it became official, but she liked the sound of it.

***

The campus felt empty, but Lauren and Adam weren't the only ones who hadn't left for home yet. They, along with Blake and Chad, had agreed to remain and work for Tony through next week, and they didn't mind. Besides needing the extra income it would provide, they were happy to help with keeping the doors of the pizza place open. With Kevin and Kerri leaving for New York on Monday and many of the other college students going home for Winter Break, Tony needed them to keep things running, and Lauren actually liked the idea of being in the college town and on the Lifegate campus for a week without any classes to attend or tests to study for.

The semester had gone okay, but she felt clueless about her future. She enjoyed the time she'd had with Adam, but it had been more limited than she would have preferred. Their schedules hadn't been very compatible, and Adam needed to work a lot. Her favorite days had been those they worked at Tony's together, even though it often left her with less time to study than she needed.

For the most part she hated school—academically speaking. She enjoyed college life, her relationship with Adam, being here with her brother and the many friends she had made, and she liked the church they attended and the ways she was involved in ministry there. But her classes had been boring and tedious. She'd gotten good grades—all A's and B's as far as she knew, but nothing had captured her interest.

If it wasn't for Adam and Blake being here, she could see herself going home for Winter Break and not coming back. She didn't know if she had a bad attitude, was burned-out on school, or if she wasn't meant to go to college, but right now it felt good to be here for work and time with Adam, rather than school. Tonight had been the last night food had been served in the dining hall, and she knew Adam felt happy about being released from that for a few weeks just as much as she felt happy about no more classes until mid January.

"What do you want to do with the rest of our evening?" Adam asked in a teasing tone. "Blake and Chad won't be back from Tony's for at least another three hours, and my other roommates are gone."

She smiled at him. "I guess you're going to be really lonely then." She faked a yawn. "I'm tired. I think I'll turn in early tonight."

He tickled her, and she squirmed away from him with a little squeal—a sound that only Adam could bring out of her. She had never been a squealer and been annoyed by girls who were—until four months ago.

"Come here, Angel," he said, pulling her back to him and promising to be good.

She snuggled into his side and had a peaceful feeling in her heart. She had been teasing about going to bed early rather than spending the evening with him, and she knew he was teasing about taking her to his room while his roommates were away. He freely admitted his weakness in that area of their relationship, but he also was doing all he could to safeguard it, and other than that one night two months ago when he had crossed the line, he'd been perfect ever since, and she felt very grateful for his faithful restraint.

"You know I'm teasing you," he said. "I wouldn't even be able to climb those stairs with you, let alone get you into my room and do something about it."

They were approaching the parking area, and she didn't know of any movies they had been told were okay to see. Adam had been really careful about that. At first she felt a little cheated out of being able to go to the movies as freely as she used to. She knew what the characters on-screen did together wasn't always right, but she felt like she could separate herself from it and make the right choices.

She had been willing to not go for Adam's sake. He found that separation between fantasy and reality more difficult. But after a couple of months of only seeing one movie, she didn't feel she was missing anything, and the purity of their relationship was worth it to her.

She had expected it to be a long and difficult battle after that night in his truck, always having to be the strong one and loving him too much to let go like she knew she should if he wasn't going to treat her right. But Adam hadn't let that happen, and she loved him even more now. She had become more convinced of his genuine love for her too. He wasn't in this just to have someone make him feel good on Friday night.

"Don't take this the wrong way," she said. "But could we stay here?"

"And do what?"

"Just talk."

"I'd like that," he said seriously. "I think The Oasis is open tonight."

"How about if we go to the lounge in my dorm," she said. "If I go to The Oasis, I'm going to want a piece of that chocolate cake they have."

"What's wrong with that?"

"I'm gaining too much weight here. Haven't you noticed?"

He glanced her over from head to toe. "No," he said. "You look just fine to me."

She had never struggled with her weight before, but here she often found comfort in food when she was feeling unsettled about her future career path or depression took over. She had wanted to talk to Adam about how she felt, but it never seemed like the right time.

"I need to talk to you about something," she said, slipping her arms around his waist and leaning her head against his chest. "And I need you to tell me what you think I should do, not just say, 'Whatever you want to do, I'll support you in that,' okay?"

"What's going on?"

She had planned to lead him inside, sit on one of the couches in front of the glowing gas fireplace, and say it calmly, like she had given it all a lot of thought, but now she just blurted it out.

"I hate school," she said. "I like being here, but I hate school."

"Like you want to drop out?" he asked.

"Maybe. I don't know. That's what I feel like doing, but I'm worried by February I'll regret it."

He led them inside then, out of the chilly air and into the warmer but still cool lounge. No one had turned on the fire tonight, and they were the only ones here. Adam flipped the switch on the wall and sat beside her. He didn't say anything for a minute, and then he asked in a strained voice, "Like you wouldn't come back next semester?"

In that moment she knew she didn't want that. Yes, she had been considering that possibility, but no, she couldn't take four months away from Adam. She would endure boring classes and stressful exams for the limited amount of time they had together. And it wasn't actually that limited—just not as much as she wanted.

"No, I'm coming back," she said. "For one more semester at least. But after that, I'm not sure. Maybe next year I'll live in town and work at Tony's full-time. Or do you think that would be a mistake?"

"I know you told me not to say this, Angel, but I think whatever you want to do is what you should do, and I will support you in anything—except living in a different state than me for half a year."

"You don't want to know what my brother has been going through, huh?"

"No, I prefer to not know that. This might sound selfish, but I need you here, Lauren. School has always been a bit of a struggle for me. I'm too lazy about it, but being here with you has brought me joy."

A thought occurred to her that completely changed her perspective on the entire thing, and a feeling of purpose and joy entered her heart. Adam needed her to be here, and that was enough of a reason to be. Maybe she wasn't meant to pursue a specific career, but Adam was, and she could be a support to him in that.

"I'm not going anywhere," she said, adjusting her position and snuggling into him. "It helps to talk about it. And you always listen to me."

"Are you thinking about next summer yet?"

"About going back to camp?"

"Yes."

"I think I want to. Do you?"

"If that's where you're going to be."

She smiled. "I know it will be tough sometimes—not having time like this together every day, but of all the things I've done in the last couple of years, being a counselor has been the most fun and rewarding for me."

"So, the idea of being involved in ministry with me, either full-time or in a volunteer capacity, like say, for the next fifty years or so—that appeals to you?"

It was the first time since this summer Adam had talked about the possibility of them spending the rest of their lives together, and she answered him seriously.

"Yes. I like the sound of that."

"Me too," he said, kissing her and taking her back to the first time he had done so. She remembered feeling very safe with him, like she could trust him to take care of her and his affection was real and genuine.

"I love you, Lauren," he whispered.

"I love you too, and I need you."

"I need you," he echoed. "You're the most special person in my life, and I don't want to let go."

"You don't have to. Just keep loving me, and I'll be here."

Chapter Twenty-Eight

Rachael felt nervous about seeing Josiah. She had been enjoying their phone conversations; he'd called her twice more since Thanksgiving, and she called him once too. And his online messages had become a daily thing. When Josiah had suggested coming to see her on his way up to Washington today, she hadn't argued for a second, but now that he was less than an hour away from actually being here, she felt like the butterflies in her stomach were having a badminton tournament.

She liked him so much, but she was afraid to hope. And even if Josiah said the feeling was mutual, she had something she needed to tell him today she feared would drive him away. She had wanted to tell him several times, but she hadn't been able to say the words, and now she feared he would see it as a betrayal on her part for keeping such vital information from him. It wasn't like they were dating, she rationalized, but in a way they had been. Even if neither of them had come out and said it, something was going on she didn't want to end, and she doubted he did either.

He arrived about the time she was expecting, and she went outside to meet him. He was planning to spend the night here, but she wanted a few minutes alone with him before he came inside to meet her family. He'd met them before when she had been dating Gabe, but she didn't know what to expect with him coming today. She was hoping for some kind of indication of that.

She hadn't seen Josiah in over a year, but he looked exactly the same. Gabe had a sophisticated look, but Josiah was more of a farm boy like she was used to around here. She remembered when she met him last summer and thought he would be perfect for her best friend, but now she wanted him all for herself.

She walked toward him on the front path and smiled. He smiled in return, and she gave him a hug like she wanted to. He held her close, and she could feel the caring in his touch like she had been hearing in his voice—verbally and written. But his words now were a little surprising.

"It's good to finally hold you," he said.

She wasn't sure what to say. "Is it?"

He stepped back suddenly. "I mean, *see* you. I meant see you."

She didn't buy it. "It's good to see you too," she laughed.

"Okay," he said, pulling her back to him. "This is good too."

The sincerity of his touch was overwhelming. She wasn't supposed to be doing this, but it felt too good, and she decided it would be better to tell him the whole truth now. If he hadn't greeted her this way, she would have been content to wait until after dinner, but since he was obviously having feelings beyond friendship, she knew it wouldn't be fair to keep it from him any longer.

"Rachael, I—"

She interrupted him. "Before you say anything, I have something I need to tell you."

He stepped back again. "What?"

"Not here. Can we go for a drive?"

"Sure," he said, appearing more curious than concerned. She knew he had no idea she was about to lay such a bombshell on him.

"Let me get my coat," she said. "You can wait for me in the car."

Going inside to get her jacket and let her mom know she was going someplace with Josiah, she told her mom he needed to go pick something up at the store. Her mom didn't question it, but Rachael knew as soon as she said it she needed to tell her the truth. There had been enough lies between them over the last six months, and she had promised herself just this morning she wasn't going to be lying to anyone anymore. Even little white lies that weren't nearly as serious as the ones she had been caught in two months ago.

"Actually, that's not true," she said to her mom whose back was turned to her while she was stirring something on the stove.

Her mom turned around. "It's not?"

"No. I need to talk to Josiah. You know, about what happened with Steven."

"I thought you already told him."

"No. I couldn't do it over the phone."

Her mom gave her a look she had seen often recently. A look of disappointment mixed with genuine love and concern. She had always known her parents loved her and were concerned about her, but them being disappointed in her was a recent thing—and they had every right to be.

She decided to be completely honest, knowing she could use her mom's support and prayers right now. Her mom had always been that way, but she hadn't appreciated it much in the past. She knew better now and hoped her mom wouldn't dash her hopes with Josiah, but she wouldn't blame her if she did. Two months ago she had made a vow to herself to not date anyone for a year until she could fully heal from what had happened with Gabe and with Steven, and yet here she was jumping at the first bright prospect to come her way.

"I like him, Mom," she admitted. "I like him a lot."

Her mom waited for her to go on.

"I know I probably shouldn't. I didn't plan for this to happen. I saw Josiah as a safe friend who was there when I needed him. But then—"

Her mom crossed the kitchen and took her into her arms. She didn't say anything, and Rachael let the tears come. "He's not going to want me after I tell him. I know it. That's why I haven't."

"You don't know that, Rachael. You *think* that," her mom said. "Just tell him, sweetie, and see what happens. The truth is better than lies even if it doesn't work out the way you hope."

"I know," she said, stepping back and drying her tears. She needed to get back out there, or Josiah would wonder what had happened to her. "Will you pray for me?"

"I always do."

"I know. Thanks."

"And Rachael?"

"Yes."

"I know you made that vow about not dating to protect yourself, but sometimes God has other ways of doing that than we do."

Her mom's words surprised her, and she smiled. "You don't even know Josiah."

"No, but I know Jesus, and I don't see it as a coincidence that Josiah's letter is what brought your relationships with both Gabe and Steven to an end—which at the time seemed devastating to you and yet has brought you back to where you need to be. And I also know these last six weeks you've been more yourself than I've seen in a long time."

She knew that was true. She felt more herself. Other than keeping the truth from Josiah about her relationship with Steven that had come to an abrupt end on the day she had received his letter, she had been completely honest with him and completely real. And it wasn't something she had to force herself to do; Josiah brought it out of her.

"But how do I know if what I feel for Josiah is any different than what I felt for Gabe and Steven? I felt this way about them too."

"It might not be any different than what you felt for Gabe and Steven. The difference will be in how Josiah responds to the way he feels about you. Will he put his own desires and needs above yours like Gabe and Steven did, or will he do things the right way?"

She knew what her mom was saying, and she nodded. "Okay. I'd better go."

Rachael stepped outside with a little more hope in her heart than she'd had five minutes ago, and it reminded her of how she felt after her mom and dad had learned the truth about her relationship with Steven. Not right away. At first she'd been very angry and tried to defend their relationship, but after a few days she felt a sense of relief they finally knew and she didn't have to keep any more secrets from them.

She had Josiah drive to the park that wasn't far from her house, and they got out to take a walk. It was cold today, but not raining. Josiah got his heavier coat to put on over his hooded gray sweatshirt, and they began walking on the paved trail. It was the first time they had ever been here together—or anywhere just the two of them—and yet it didn't feel that way. She felt like they'd been friends for a long time.

"I have something serious to tell you, and I want you to know I never would have kept this from you if I would have known I'd be having such strong feelings for you right now."

"How are you feeling?" he asked.

She stopped and looked at him, knowing she had to be honest about that too. "Like I'm falling in love with you. Are you feeling that way too, or did I read too much into your hug back at the house?"

"No, you didn't," he said, reaching for her and pulling her close to him. "But I thought it was just me."

"It's not," she said, letting him hold her for a moment but then stepping back and feeling like this was the hardest thing she would ever have to do in her life. "You're making me feel like I used to before my life got so messed up."

"Before you got my letter?"

"No, before that."

He didn't seem to follow, and she knew why. "I shouldn't have kept this from you, Josiah, but I was so ashamed. I had another relationship—before I learned the truth about Gabe."

"When?"

"Over the summer and up until the day I got your letter."

"With who?"

Rachael took a deep breath and breathed a silent prayer. This was the tough part. "With my track coach."

"From high school?"

"Yes. He was my track coach all four years. He's a math teacher there too."

"How old is he?"

"Twenty-seven."

Josiah didn't respond but didn't appear too alarmed—yet. There was one more significant detail.

"And, he's married," she confessed. "He's separated from his wife right now. He was before the summer. They split up during track season, and that's kind of how something got started between us."

Chapter Twenty-Nine

Josiah listened as Rachael explained in detail the last six months of her life. Track was her forte, and she had always loved it. She'd gone to the state championships the last three years and had placed well in the 400 and 800 this past spring. Her running coach had helped her to improve over her four years of high school, and they'd always had that student-teacher relationship until this spring when he was going through some tough personal things and she began spending time with him after practice and other times too.

Steven and his wife had separated, and he'd opened up to her emotionally, and she'd listened. He told her several times, 'I shouldn't be talking to you about this,' but she kept telling him it was okay, even though she knew it probably wasn't the best thing for him to be confiding in a student and spending so much time with her outside of school. It had started innocent enough with her helping him put equipment away after practice and him walking her to her car after everyone else had left. But then she'd gone out to dinner with him one night and then again a week later. She told her mom and dad she had gone to the library because she knew they wouldn't approve of her spending time with him like that, even if it was perfectly innocent.

She had talked with him about Gabe and shared with him she felt like things were over between them even though they hadn't officially ended things. She hadn't told him or anyone about the real reason behind Gabe's apparent loss of interest in her. She told her coach what she told everyone else—that they were thinking of going to different colleges and that maybe having a long-distance relationship with each other wasn't going to work out. But Steven had said all the right things about there being someone else out there for her: that she was a very pretty and special girl who could have anyone she wanted.

She had been flattered by his words and started to develop a serious crush on him, even though he was technically still married. She rationalized it by telling herself he was probably going to end up divorced and the majority of their problems had to do with his wife, not him, and they were just spending innocent time together anyway.

"After graduation I didn't see him until two weeks later. I had gone to the school to run, and he was there. I had just heard about Gabe going into the Air Force, and I was debating about what I was going to do. In a way I think I decided to hold on to Gabe instead of just breaking it off because I knew Steven was starting to have feelings for me, and the only defense I had against doing something I knew wasn't right was that I had a boyfriend. The fact he was my coach, technically still married, and ten years older than me wasn't enough to keep me from allowing anything to happen between us, but I couldn't cheat on Gabe—at least not right then."

Josiah had a sinking feeling this story had a bad ending, but he needed to hear it. His hopes of having Rachael in his life were deflating rapidly, but he couldn't say, 'Stop! I don't want to hear any more,' and walk away. He was a part of this now, and he needed to see it through, whatever the outcome may be.

"When did things start to happen?"

"I saw him three or four times a week for most of the summer. Usually he would meet me after I got off work and we would go somewhere—either out to dinner in out-of-the-way places or we would go for a drive somewhere. Nobody knew about it. Not even my friends. We kept telling ourselves we weren't doing anything wrong, but we didn't want anyone to know—I knew it wasn't right, but I wanted that time with him."

"Were you just friends or more than that?"

"At first we were just friends, but then one day in late July we went to the beach together, and I told him I was planning to break up with Gabe because I hadn't heard from him and felt like it was over. He admitted he really liked me, and he told me everything I wanted to hear about Gabe being a jerk and what a great person I was—the kind of girl he wished he would have married instead of his wife. And then he kissed me. After that, things were pretty much the same between us, but slowly we got more physical. I started going over to his apartment because I was afraid of someone catching us kissing somewhere else."

She stopped walking and looked up at him. The shame and embarrassment was written all over her face. "Josiah, if you've heard enough, you can take me home and get on with your life. I can stand here and make excuses for myself all night, but I know what I did was really stupid—and wrong. I was cheating on Gabe, and allowing Steven to cheat on his wife, and lying to my parents—" Her voice broke, but she continued. "And now I've been lying to you all this time—I should have told you before now. I'm sorry."

Josiah had a couple of questions he wanted to know the answers to before he made any kind of decision, and he also had an incredible desire to be a friend to Rachael right now. He wasn't sure why, he just did, and technically that's all they were.

She hadn't made any kind of commitment to him that would require her to tell him all of this before now, and he hadn't been entirely honest with her these last six weeks either. He'd been attracted to girls before, but not like this, and he knew he should have told her about the strong feelings going on in his heart before now. Even today he hadn't been fully prepared to do that until a slip of the tongue had given him away and he'd had no choice but to be honest after that.

"You don't have to be sorry, Rachael," he said, taking her into his arms and giving her a long hug. "We all make mistakes. And I know this has been a tough year for you."

"Don't make excuses for me, Josiah."

"I'm not making excuses. Just tell me everything right now, and I promise that you'll at least have my friendship, okay?"

"Okay," she said, stepping back and wiping her nose with a tissue.

"Can I ask you something?"

"Yes."

"Were you having sex with him?"

"No," she said. "I couldn't rationalize that much— even on the day I got your letter."

"You saw him that day?"

"Yes. I wasn't supposed to. It was a Thursday, and we didn't usually see each other because he had cross-country meets after school, and I was helping with the children's choir at church in the evening, but after I got the letter from you, I was really upset and felt like I needed to see him, so I told my mom I wasn't feeling well and stayed home from church that night, but I went over to Steven's apartment after my parents left.

"It all hurt so much, and I was ready to be with Steven and let his love take my pain away, but then I couldn't, and Steven knew I wasn't in a good place emotionally, so he didn't try to force anything. We ended up just talking and then when I was rushing to make it home on time so my parents wouldn't know I had been out, I pulled out of the apartment complex and smashed into an oncoming car."

"And that's how your mom and dad found out?"

"Yes. Steven didn't see the accident, but he heard it and came out to see if it was me. He was at the hospital when my mom and dad got there, and he told them everything."

"Have you seen him since?"

"Only once. My mom and dad didn't forbid me from seeing him, but they strongly advised me to end it, and I knew they were right. He was good to me, honestly, but I know he's meant to be with his wife, and I'm meant to be with someone else. We both allowed our emptiness in other areas of our life to bring us together instead of trying to work through our own individual problems. It was like trying to put a Band-Aid on some really serious wounds."

***

The shame of what she had allowed to happen hit Rachael afresh once again as she spilled the whole story to Josiah, but she also felt grateful God had kept her from making more serious mistakes and rescued her from the lies and secrets she hadn't been able to get out of herself. It seemed unreal in a way, like a weird dream, and yet it had been very real. Her hurt over Gabe turning on her the way he had, the strong feelings she had developed for a married man, and Josiah's letter that had brought that phase of her life to an official and abrupt end.

"In a strange way, Gabe's mistakes actually led to my benefit," she said.

"How's that?"

She smiled at him. "If he would have told me the truth himself, I probably would have ended up with Steven sooner, and I never would have gotten a letter from you. I could still be with him now."

"I think God would have rescued you in another way."

"Yes, but I like this way. You've been a really great friend to me, Josiah, and I'm very grateful for that. Even if you tell me good-bye tonight and I never see you again, you've made a difference in my life. The way you've encouraged me in my faith these last two months—I can't even tell you how much your words have meant to me."

"How are you?" he asked, sounding genuinely concerned about her, just like always. "Really. You don't have to pretend with me, Rachael."

"Much better than I was two months ago," she said. "I have good days and not so good days, but I'm trying really hard to believe God still loves me and I'm forgiven and He can make something good out of all of this."

"It sounds like someone has been giving you good advice."

She smiled. "I've appreciated every word, Josiah. Honestly. I can't imagine doing as well as I am right now if I didn't have your friendship and support. I feel guilty because you've thought I was so innocent in all of this, but I couldn't tell you and risk losing you. I hope you can forgive me for that. I told God this morning, 'No more lies. No more secrets. Just honesty.' And so far today, He's helped me to do that. I even told my mom about you before I left—I mean, she already knew about you, but I was honest with her about wanting you as more than a friend."

He didn't seem opposed to that, but he appeared to be thinking something, so she waited for him to voice his thoughts. She had told him everything she needed to say.

"Would it be all right if we went back and had dinner with your family and then talked more later?" he asked.

"Kind of overwhelming to hear all at once, huh?"

"Not so much that," he said. "It's just most of our time together has been a lot of talking—in one form or another—and I want time with you in normal life. Having dinner with your family and being with you. Is that okay?"

Remembering what her mom had said about the way Josiah responded to the feelings she had for him, she felt even more convinced Josiah was exactly what she needed: a guy who wanted to be a part of her normal life, not sneaking in time with her on the side or just communicating from a distance.

"I'd like that," she said.

He drove them back, and they went inside. Her parents hadn't eaten yet and seemed pleased Josiah was with her. They welcomed him easily, and Josiah acted happy to meet them again in a different capacity than before. When Josiah asked where the bathroom was and left them momentarily, Rachael helped with setting the food on the table, and her mom asked how things had gone, and she shared her honest thoughts.

"He's still here," she said. "But I think it's going to take some time to sink in for him."

"How long do you think he'll stay?"

"I have no idea. I'll just leave that up to him."

After dinner they spent time talking at the table with her mom and dad, and then her parents gave them privacy together in the formal living room. Josiah asked her why she had called him that first time, and she was honest with him. She had called him initially to thank him for the letter like she told him that day, but there was another reason she hadn't shared with him yet.

"That morning at church I had surrendered myself to God completely, telling Him to guide my steps and I would do whatever He told me to do. And I didn't hear Him telling me anything specific until that afternoon when I reread your letter. There were some things I hadn't noticed before, but they stood out to me because your words about clinging to God and believing He had a perfect plan matched what my pastor had said. And then I heard Him saying, 'Call Josiah.' So I did."

"Did He keep telling you to call me after that?"

"Yes. I knew I needed you for a friend and He had brought you into my life at just the right time. You were the first person I told the truth to about the real reason behind why Gabe didn't want me anymore, and after that I felt like I could tell you anything. Except about Steven—and that was only because I was so ashamed and afraid you wouldn't want to talk to me anymore, and I couldn't handle that."

"I would have still been your friend, Rachael."

"I know, and if your friendship is all you can give me now, that's enough, Josiah. Honestly."

He turned his body to face her more and reached out to stroke her cheek. "I have a confession of my own to make." He dropped his hand from her face and laid it over her fingers. "I didn't expect you to call me after you got the letter. I thought you might write me back to let me know you got it and to tell me how you were doing, but after I talked to you that first night, I really hoped you would call again, and as soon as you did, I was gone after that. I don't talk to girls as easily as I can talk to you, and I knew you needed me, and that was a good feeling."

She smiled. "And that was real, Josiah. I did need you. And I couldn't let go of that."

"If I ask you something, will you give me an honest answer?"

"Yes."

"Do you think it would be better for you if we remained friends for now with the possibility of something more down the road, or if we took that step now?"

She thought seriously about her answer, but she wasn't sure she could know that yet. This had been an emotional evening, and right now she wanted Josiah to kiss her, but maybe she wasn't ready for that. But then again, if he left tomorrow without them acting on the feelings they had for each other, that could be hard on her in another way.

She didn't feel like she deserved him, and talking herself out of what she wanted could lead her into another relationship with someone who wouldn't be what she needed. She could justify settling for less than the best much easier than accepting the incredible gift sitting right in front of her.

"Can you spend the day with me tomorrow, or do you need to get home?"

"I can stay," he said. "For more than tomorrow if you want."

"I liked what you said earlier about wanting time with me in real, everyday life. I think I need that before I can answer your question."

"Sounds like a good way to start Winter Break to me."

She smiled. "Me too."

"Is there anything else you need to tell me, Rachael? Anything at all?"

She searched her heart. Had she left anything out? She didn't think so. "No, that's everything."

"And how does that make you feel—to not have any secrets between us?"

She smiled. "Free and alive."

"I want you to be that way tomorrow, okay? No guilt. No regret. Just be free and alive with me."

"Do you forgive me, Josiah?"

"Yes. And I want you to forgive yourself."

He took her hands, kissed her on the forehead, and whispered words from the Bible he often wrote at the end of his messages:

"May the LORD bless you and keep you, Rachael. May He make His face shine upon you and give you peace."

Chapter Thirty

On Saturday morning Matt slept in. He'd gotten home late from the concert with the youth group last night. He had arranged with Pastor John to have the rest of this weekend off because of Ben and Hope's wedding today and wanting to spend time with his friends who were back in town.

Before heading out to meet Amanda at her house, he stopped at the mall to pick up something he'd had his eye on for a few weeks now. Last month when he'd gone to the jewelry store to get something for their six-month anniversary, he bought her a necklace, but he had also been drawn to the rings, and one had stood out to him he couldn't stop thinking about.

He felt a little panicked it would be gone by now. He would have bought it sooner, but he didn't have enough money. Yesterday was payday, and he hoped with all of his heart the ring hadn't been picked up by someone else. He wanted to give it to her as an engagement ring for Christmas.

When he saw it, his heart started beating more wildly than it already was. The small ring wasn't as fancy or expensive as a lot of the rings in the case, but he thought Amanda would really like it, and he couldn't afford the others. He would rather get her this now than save up for something he didn't know if she would like any better and have to wait six more months to know where his heart was.

His phone rang as he was leaving the store with the ring in his possession, and it was her. She was checking to see what time he was coming, and he told her he was on his way. They had seen each other yesterday, and every day this week, but she sounded anxious to see him anyway, and he felt the same way.

"What are you going to do with having me around so much?" he said. "You're usually free of me on the weekends."

"I'm going to enjoy every minute. I miss you already."

"I miss you too, sweetheart. Half an hour. I'll be there."

"Don't rush. I want you here in one piece."

"And what are you going to do with me when I get there?"

"Take you to a wedding."

"Ours?"

She laughed. "No, not ours. Unless you have something planned I don't know about."

"Maybe I do," he said.

"I wouldn't be surprised."

He smiled and decided right then he was going to give her the ring tonight instead of waiting until Christmas. She might be expecting that, but he could add the element of surprise tonight. "Forty-five minutes, tops," he said. "And before the wedding, I get some kisses."

***

Imagining her brother's upcoming wedding the last few months, Amber had often thought of what hers might be like, and she had been doing that all morning now that they were here. Plans had begun to form more fully in her mind, and she wanted to discuss details with Seth and her parents while they were home on break. Her mind was really racing today, from what her dress would look like, to little details Hope was dealing with like which earrings to wear and if she should wear her dress away from the church, or take clothes to change into before they left for the beach.

Amber hadn't thought that far ahead, but she had decided who she wanted in her wedding, and she definitely wanted an outdoor wedding like they had talked about, but she was prepared to get married at the church if it ended up being a rainy day. Hope had made everything really beautiful inside in mostly simple and inexpensive ways. She had chosen red and white as her colors because it was close to Christmas, and everything, including the dresses, flowers, and candles were all well coordinated.

Once Ben and Hope's ceremony got underway, she forgot about her own wedding plans and focused on the two special people in her life getting married today. It was a simple wedding. She was the Maid of Honor, and one of Ben's longtime friends was the Best Man. Two of Hope's cousins lit the candles, and Pastor Cooke performed the ceremony, mixing in elements of humor and complete seriousness about Ben and Hope's relationship and what was taking place today.

Amber couldn't help but think of all that had brought them to this day. It had been a long road for Hope, but her happiness and complete healing was unmistakable. Amber had often wondered why Hope had to go through such horrendous circumstances to bring her to a point of complete redemption, but today she could think of one reason. Her joy was complete because she wasn't taking anything for granted. God had done an incredible work in her heart, and no one knew it better than she did.

After the ceremony Amber gave them both a long hug but had to allow others to have their turn. She went to find Seth and found him not far away. Giving him a sweet kiss, she heard him say something she never got tired of hearing. "I love you, sweetheart. You look beautiful."

"Thank you."

Someone else caught her attention, and she turned to see Mandy, whom she hadn't seen since getting back. She felt tears stinging her eyes. She had missed her even more than she realized until now.

"Don't go anywhere," she commanded. "We want the rest of the day with you two."

She gave Matt a hug and whispered something in his ear. "Thanks for taking good care of her."

"That's what I promised you," he said.

Stacey and Kenny were there too along with Colleen, Nikki and Spencer, Lora and Eric, and some others from camp. They all hung out at the church until Ben and Hope left and then decided to go out for an early dinner before those who had driven a long distance had to head back.

She got in some time with Lora while she could, and she and Eric seemed very happy together. She told them their tentative wedding plans and said they would be getting an invitation.

"We'll be there," Lora said. "If you need anything, call me."

Amber enjoyed seeing all of her friends again, but the time she enjoyed the most was when it was just her and Seth with Matt and Mandy that evening. Watching Matt with Mandy and hearing him say things that truly warmed her heart about his steady and transforming relationship with Jesus, Amber thought the same thing about him as she had been thinking about Hope during the wedding.

There had been times when she had been so worried for Hope—that she would stop believing in God's love for her and plummet down to where she'd once been. And there had been times she thought Matt would never rise above his mistakes and bad choices and be the guy sitting before her right now— the guy she always knew he could be. But here he was, happier and more settled than he had been this summer before his brother's accident.

They left Mandy's house at nine-thirty and drove back to hers where they stayed up after her parents went to bed, sitting in front of the glowing fireplace like old times and sharing similar thoughts about Matt and Mandy, Ben and Hope, and their upcoming wedding. Seth wanted the same things she did, and he had some good ideas she liked. They wrote things down they could take care of while they were here, and then Seth set the to-do list aside.

She always felt safe with Seth, but especially here, and he kissed her like he hadn't while they had been away at school together. It gave her a mental picture of what things would be like between them after they were married, and her desire for him didn't surprise or scare her. She was ready to be with him, and yet she wanted to wait for the right time, and she knew Seth did too.

Before she had to ask him, Seth replaced his intense kissing with snuggling, and he expressed his desire for her verbally, using words he hadn't used before but she liked hearing and didn't feel threatened by or uncomfortable with. She knew he was simply being honest, not trying to suggest they cross any of the boundaries they had already set for themselves.

"I want to be with you, Amber. I want it more every single day."

She didn't respond or feel the need to. But she closed her eyes and allowed herself to imagine it as much as she could. She didn't know exactly what it would be like, but she knew with Seth it would be great—in whatever specific ways they expressed their love.

They sat there in silence for several minutes, and she knew Seth would be sending her off to bed soon, but when he spoke again it wasn't about that or his physical desire for her. He had something to tell her on a different subject.

"Guess what?"

"What?"

"Matt got Mandy a ring."

She looked up and smiled. "He did?"

"Yep. He picked it up this morning, and he's giving it to her tonight."

"Tonight? He's not waiting until Christmas?"

"He wants to surprise her, and he's afraid he's given her too many hints to wait until then."

"Do you think he's ready to be engaged?"

"I think so. He's had a lot of pain and difficulty this year. I told him not to be afraid of the joy."

***

Kerri was in the middle of making a Tony's Special when she felt Kevin come up behind her and slip his arms around her waist. She looked up at him and smiled. "What are you doing?"

"What are you doing? Who orders a Tony's Special at ten-thirty?"

She looked at the slip that was for a delivery order. "Curtis."

"Figures," he said. "And you're short one pepperoni."

"Too bad," she said. "This is not your area tonight. You aren't burning the last one I made, are you?"

"I never burn a pizza."

Kevin gave her sweet kisses on her neck that was exposed because of her hair being up in a ponytail. He wasn't usually affectionate with her in the kitchen, but they were the only ones here currently. It was a slow night for a Saturday.

"I love you, Kerri," he said. "I'm really glad you stayed."

"Me too," she laughed. "But that tickles."

"What's going on in here?"

Kerri turned to see Chad had come back from what should have been the last delivery for the night, but Curtis had called at ten twenty-eight. Two minutes before the delivery order cutoff time.

"I've got one more for you here, Chad. Sorry."

"That's all right," he said, coming over to look at the slip. "Ah, Curtis. He tips good."

"What are you going to do with all this extra money?" she said. "Jessica's not here for you to spoil this weekend."

"Your boyfriend is taking you to New York for Christmas, and I've got my own plans for my girl."

"Oh, yeah? Feel like sharing?" she asked, topping the pizza off with another layer of cheese and then stepping to the side to let Kevin take it to the oven.

"If you can keep a secret."

"I'm going to New York in two days, and she's already in Portland, I think you can trust me."

"There's a certain dress she's had her eye on in the boutique, and I thought I'd get it for her so she'll have something new to wear when we go to the ballet."

"The ballet? Whoa. She'll love that."

"I hope so," he said.

"I know so," she laughed, stepping over to give him a hug.

He sighed. "Why me, Kerri?"

She stepped back and gave him an honest and adamant response. "Why not! If I had picked someone for Jessie myself, I couldn't have done any better. And you know me well enough to know I wouldn't say that if it wasn't the absolute truth. You just need to wake up to what Jessie and the rest of us see so plainly, Chad."

Chapter Thirty-One

Josiah didn't think he'd ever had a more perfect day. He hadn't imagined spending today with Rachael at all, let alone having it go so well. The way she opened up to him amazed him. It had been amazing him for the last six weeks, and today he knew what had started between them over the phone and online had been real. He didn't feel like he was falling in love with the idea of her. He wanted to love her, and putting her at the center of his world would be very easy to do.

He'd never been in love, so he didn't know exactly what it was supposed to feel like, but this wasn't like anything he had ever experienced. It wasn't the same as when he'd been attracted to girls in the past. It wasn't about fleeting thoughts and momentary pleasure, but something deeper. Rachael made him feel more alive somehow, and he cared for her on a subconscious level. He wasn't thinking to himself, 'Okay, I need to say this or that, or do this or that for her,' but when she seemed happy, he felt that way too, and when the memory of her mistakes returned, he felt her pain. When he could see she needed a hug, he gave her one, and when she needed a good tickling, he gave her that too.

He had decided by midday he wanted to stay through tomorrow, and he hoped she would be okay with that. He thought she would be, especially as the evening came and he could tell she wasn't ready for their time together to be over.

After dinner with her family, he decided to put her out of her misery and tell her what he was thinking so she wouldn't have to ask. She had helped her mom clear away the dishes while he was talking to her dad, and then she sat down beside him at the empty table as her mom and dad left the room and said they were going to the church for a little while to set up some things for Sunday morning. Her mom and dad were in charge of the children's ministry program at the church, and they were having their annual children's choir performance tomorrow during the regular church service.

"Do you need help?" Rachael asked.

"No, the Larsons are going to be there. We shouldn't be too long."

After they were gone, Josiah moved his chair closer to hers and leaned over to whisper his inquiry in her ear. "Would it be all right if I went to church with you in the morning and then spent the rest of the day here?"

She smiled. "Yes."

"Has this been a good day for you?"

"Yes."

He reached for her hand. "Just okay, or really good?"

"Really good."

"Me too," he said.

"Why has this been a good day for you?"

"Because I've spent it with you."

"And what was good about that?" she inquired further.

"Everything," he said honestly. "When I'm with you, a piece that's been missing in my heart is suddenly there. I've been feeling that way every time I talked to you, and today it's like that times a thousand."

"I feel that way too," she said in a peaceful way. "When I'm with you, I feel like everything is going to be okay."

Josiah had never kissed a girl before, and whenever he had imagined kissing a girl, it had always been more about the desire he had. He wanted to kiss someone because he was attracted to her and wanted to act on that attraction. And he felt that way about Rachael too, but he also felt something else. He wanted to kiss her to let her know he cared for her and he was someone she could trust with her fragile heart.

"Have you thought any more about the question I asked you last night?" he asked first.

"Yes," she replied.

"If you don't have an answer for me yet, it's fine. But do you?"

She smiled. "Yes, I think I do."

"Do you want to tell me?"

"If you want me to."

"I want you to."

She sat back in her chair and let out a happy sigh. "I want this, Josiah. I feel like I totally don't deserve it, but I can't push you away or put my feelings on hold. You're the nicest, sweetest guy I've ever met, and you know about my mistakes but you're treating me like I never made them."

"You have a pure heart, Rachael. Two men abused that, but they can't take it away from you, and that's what I see."

"Thank you," she whispered.

"May I kiss you?"

She smiled. "Yes."

He felt his heart pounding as he leaned forward and gently kissed her lips. When he opened his eyes and saw her smiling at him, he kissed her again, and it felt too easy and right to be a mistake.

"I want this too, Rachael," he said softly. "I want you and me to be you and me. For a long time."

Tears welled up in her eyes and slipped onto her delicate skin. He held her close, gently stroking her back and wishing so much he could erase all of her pain.

"I mean it, Rachael. I'm not going anywhere. I'm not going to ask you to do things that aren't right, and I'm going to take care of you—not just talk about it, but actually do it."

"I know you will," she said, holding him tighter.

He kissed her again, honestly trying to convey his deep affection for her and feeling hers for him in return. It was amazing and made him feel lightheaded and dizzy. After waiting so long to have a girl return his interest in her, it was a little overwhelming, especially since Rachael was such a beautiful woman and he suddenly felt more like a man than a boy. He had been surprised when her parents left them here alone together, and now he was thinking, 'How could they do that? What parents in their right mind would trust me alone with their beautiful and vulnerable daughter?'

They're trusting you, Josiah, and so is Rachael. Don't abuse that.

Slowly he pulled away and felt the need to be honest. "Wow, that feels good in a hurry, doesn't it?"

"Yes," she said. "You've never kissed anyone like that?"

"I've never kissed anyone, period."

"No way."

He didn't respond.

"Josiah!" She laughed. "You're kidding me!"

"Nope, you're my first. I hope I wasn't too awful at it."

She laughed again. "Definitely not. If that was your first try, I'm in major trouble."

He smiled. He thought it had been pretty great, but it was nice to hear she thought so too. "Come here," he said, standing up from his chair and taking her by the hand.

"Where are we going?" she asked, following him out of the kitchen and toward the stairs.

He thought about taking her upstairs to give her something he had bought for her, but he decided against it. Sending her into the living room while he went upstairs, he found the jewelry case in the side pocket of his duffel bag and took it downstairs with him but held it behind his back as he entered the formal living room where Rachael had taken a seat on the smaller sofa.

"Close your eyes," he said, sitting beside her and seeing her do as he asked. Her delightful expression as she patiently waited was too beautiful to resist, and he gave her a soft kiss.

He pulled the box from behind his back and held it between them, opening the case and hoping she liked what he had selected. He'd bought the set of purity jewelry from the campus bookstore this week after he knew he was going to be seeing her. Seth had advised him to think ahead, and he thought his roommate was crazy to think there would be a need for it this soon, even if by some miracle she allowed him to kiss her, but now he knew Seth was exactly right. A commitment to purity was not something to be delayed. He needed the reminder now, and Rachael needed the added security she could trust him.

"If you hate it, just say so, and I can get you something else, okay?"

"May I open my eyes?"

"Yes."

She did, and her eyes fell on the open case in his hands. She didn't say anything, but her eyes filled with tears. Looking up at him, she smiled. "When did you get that?"

"On Thursday. Do you like it?"

"Are you kidding? I love it! They're beautiful."

There was a necklace, a bracelet, and a ring. All of them had the words Love, Trust, and Purity etched into the silver metal. He took the ring from the center and asked if he could put it on her now. She extended her fingers, and he slipped it into place.

Rachael stared at it for a moment and then gave him a hug. "Where did you come from?" she whispered. "How is this happening to me?"

"It should have happened the first time around. This is what you deserve. This is the way you should be treated."

"I guess God knew what He was doing after all," she said.

He sat back and looked at her, wiping away her tears with his fingers. "About what?"

"I asked Him so many times, 'Why did you bring Gabe into my life if he wasn't the right guy for me?' But now I know why. I met him so I could meet you, and so I would appreciate you that much more."

"Don't be putting too much faith in me," he said. "Giving you this stuff and actually living it are two different things."

"And asking God for someone like you and actually having you are two different things, but it's happening."

Knowing he was an answer to her prayers gave Josiah a different view of himself and of Rachael. He had always seen himself as shy and ordinary, and he'd seen Rachael as a girl who had it all together and could take care of herself and didn't want or need a guy like him. But she did, and if she needed him to take care of her, that's what he would do.

He kissed her again and slowly allowed the level of passion to increase, but he didn't cross any lines he knew he shouldn't.

"I think I like this better than the phone," he said.

"I'm glad you're staying one more day."

"Do you want me to stay more? I can."

"I want you to stay as long as you want to stay."

"Your parents would start charging me rent if I did that."

He kissed her more but knew he couldn't spend the whole time until her parents returned doing that. And remembering what Seth had told him about getting into the habit of showing Rachael affection when others were around, not just when he had her all to himself, he knew he didn't have to take advantage of this alone-time they had. If they didn't have anything to hide, then he didn't have to. There would be plenty of opportunities to let Rachael know how he felt about her and enjoy her sweet touch—whether they were alone or had others among them.

He shifted his position, sitting back against the sofa and pulling her gently against him. Kissing was nice, but holding her had an appeal all its own, and she seemed to enjoy the feeling also.

"What was your favorite part of today?" he asked.

"Besides right now?"

"Yes."

She answered without hesitation. "That hour we spent walking around the OSU campus talking about God."

He had enjoyed that too. It had been totally spontaneous. She'd made a comment about what she had read while doing her devotions last night after they'd said good night to each other, and a whole conversation about their current relationships with God had spilled from it. Both of them were on the same path of getting to know God on a deeply personal level, but their ways of getting there had been different, so Josiah felt like they could learn a lot from each other's experiences.

Rachael had taken the harder road, learning things through the pain caused by others and her own mistakes, while he had been more consistent in believing God and doing things the right way and seeing God be faithful to bless him for it. But Rachael had been blessed too—by seeing the grace of God that could help her overcome her mistakes and see God use them for good once she surrendered herself to Him instead of trying to work things out her own way.

"I liked that too," he said. "And I want that to be a big part of our relationship. You can tell me anything, even if you feel mad at God or frustrated by how He's working."

"I felt that way for a long time without realizing it."

"Do you feel that way now?"

"No, not right now. I'm sure I'll feel that way at times in the future when different struggles come my way, but right now I can see that God knew exactly what He was doing, and I couldn't be more thankful."

Chapter Thirty-Two

After Amber and Seth left the house, Matt knew the time he had been waiting for had arrived. Having told Seth his plans to ask Mandy to marry him and receiving his friend's support, Matt knew it was definitely the right time. He'd also talked to Amanda's dad this afternoon and had received the go-ahead from him, but one thing concerned him. The size of the ring. When he had seen it in the display case at the store, he could imagine it on Amanda's delicate and slender finger just fine. But after seeing the ring Seth had gotten for Amber and Ben had gotten for Hope, it seemed very small in comparison, and he felt embarrassed about giving her something that said, 'My fiancé is poor and can only afford this dinky little ring.'

But it wasn't just the ring. It was the reality he had no real way to support himself and Amanda as soon as this summer. His internship at the church didn't pay enough, and finding a second job would leave little room for college. He would be married to Amanda but never see her. His one consolation was that her education was already paid for, so he wouldn't be holding her back from pursuing her dreams, but maybe it would be better to wait.

If he hadn't already talked to her dad this afternoon, he would have no problem with putting his plans on hold, but her dad had seemed very supportive, agreeing to help them out with whatever they needed, but Matt didn't know if he felt comfortable with that. Maybe he needed to think this through more.

Stepping back inside the house and closing the door, he was caught off-guard by Amanda's behavior. Over the last few months she had become increasingly confident in the belief he was attracted to her in every way, and he had a weakness for a certain look she gave him. After spending most of the day surrounded by other people and attending a wedding, he should have been prepared for it now that it was just the two of them, but he wasn't. His mind had been on the ring and the words he wanted to say. Amanda, however, was oblivious to any such plans and seemed to have her own agenda for the rest of this evening.

"Don't look at me that way," he said, "or I'm sending you straight to bed."

She smiled a bit, only making it worse, and he had no choice but to steer her away from the secluded alcove at the front of the house to the living area where her family was still talking. But once they were seated on the couch beside her grandmother, Amanda simply snuggled into his side, and he couldn't do anything besides hold her equally in return.

He was so completely in love with her that her happiness had become his own. If she was happy, he was happy. If she was unhappy, which was rare these days, he couldn't let her remain there. Her contentment usually equaled his own, but tonight he felt unsettled. He had felt so confident of his decision this morning and for most of the day, but now he wasn't sure.

He wasn't surprised when her parents and grandmother and older brother announced they were going to bed at ten. He was tempted to say he was tired and suggest they go to bed too, but he knew without having to ask she wanted more time with him, and not taking that time would be rare. He loved their times of complete aloneness. He craved them. And it wasn't about having the chance to kiss and hold her more freely than when others were surrounding them.

He had been doing all right today with it being a happy occasion and having old friends to hang out with, but now that everyone was gone, he realized how much he needed her all to himself. Even at the end of an otherwise perfect day.

He wasn't sure if he was going to give her the ring tonight or wait, but he felt like kissing her, and so he did. She seemed more needy than usual, and he couldn't do anything less than kiss her the way he knew she wanted to be kissed. Soft and passionate. Loving and intimate. It was a perfect mix of desire and affection—something he knew God had given him the ability to balance just right. He enjoyed the moment right along with her, not feeling like he could lose control at any second. He knew what he was doing. He was loving her, and it felt right and satisfying for what it was.

"Do you love me, Amanda?" he asked, leaning his forehead against hers and stroking her cheek with his fingertips.

"Yes."

"Why?"

She smiled. "Because I can't help it."

He kissed her more and knew the same was true for him. He couldn't help but love her. But was his love enough? Didn't she need more from him? What if he couldn't take care of her? What if he let her down? He didn't think he could bear it.

"I have something to ask you," he said. "Something serious, and I want you to be completely honest with me, okay?"

"Okay," she said easily, as if he was about to ask what she wanted to do tomorrow.

"Is there any chance you could marry me this summer?"

She smiled. "Yes."

"Yes? Just like that?"

"Yes."

"Why? I'm poor, directionless, and completely pathetic."

She laughed. "No, you're not."

"I am, Amanda," he said, sitting back and distancing himself from her loving touch. "Give me one good reason why you could marry me, and none of this 'just because'."

"Because you love me."

"There's more to love than just saying the words."

"So, you don't love me?" she said, playfully kissing his cheek. "You just say that to get good kisses?" She turned his face toward her and gave him another kiss on the lips.

"Amanda," he said between kisses. "I'm serious."

She sat back and gave him a curious look. "Matthew? What are you trying to say? Whatever it is, just say it so we can get back to kissing. I've been waiting all day for this."

He said it. "I want to marry you."

"This summer?"

"Yes."

She smiled. "Okay."

"That's insane!"

"So, you don't want to?"

"No, I want to, but it's insane. Talk me out of it. Tell me to ask again when I have direction for my life, money in the bank, and a plan for how to take care of you."

"That sounds boring."

"It sounds wise and practical and—"

"And like too long to wait. It could be ten years before you figure all that out."

"See, you do think I'm pathetic."

"No, I think you're Matthew Abramson, the man I love and want to spend the rest of my life with. You're real. You love me. And you—"

"Spent most of my paycheck to buy you a ring?"

"What?" She laughed.

"You heard me."

"Where is it?"

"Right here," he said, pulling the tissue he'd wrapped it in out of his pocket and feeling like he was making the most unromantic proposal ever. His opinion changed slightly when he revealed the simple ring and saw the look of touched surprise on Amanda's face.

"Oh, Matthew. It's beautiful."

"It's tiny."

She smiled. "It's perfect."

"Really?"

"Really," she said, touching his face and giving him a tender kiss. "I love you."

"I love you too," he whispered, feeling overcome with emotion at the trusting look in her eyes and the inadequate feeling in his heart.

She held out her hand, and he took her fingers. "Are you sure, Amanda? I can wait."

"I can't," she said. "I miss you so much as it is. I want you every day. I need you every day."

He felt very unsure of his ability to make this happen and yet completely sure he wanted to, so he placed the ring on her finger, knowing he was taking a big leap of faith but it was a leap he was meant to take.

"This is crazy," he said, closing his eyes, finding her familiar lips, and kissing them with more passion and tenderness than ever.

"We'll be all right, Matthew," she said, moving to sit on his lap and giving him a hug. "It's not about what we can do. It's about what God can do for us. He'll take care of us."

"You were around Seth too much today."

"No, I've been around *you* for the last four months."

"You don't actually listen to all the stuff I say, do you?"

"When it's good stuff? Yes!"

"I'm scared, Amanda. What if I'm wrong about how I feel God leading me? What if I'm not the right guy for you?"

"You're not wrong."

"I feel completely unworthy of you. How can it be right?"

"And I'm completely in love with you. How can it be wrong?"

Kissing her once again, he put his doubts and fears aside and lived in the reality of the moment. He loved her. He'd asked her to marry him. She'd said yes.

"I'm sorry this wasn't very romantic. I saw it going differently in my head."

"It was sincere. That's better than romantic."

"We're getting married, Amanda."

"I know. Who else knows?"

"Seth and your dad for sure, and whoever they've told."

"Can I say one thing?"

"Anything, baby."

"I think we should go to Lifegate next year."

"I do too," he said. "I'm not sure how I'm going to pay for it, but I guess I'll let God take care of that. I'm so far out on a limb with Him already, what's one more thing?"

*I'd love to hear how God has used
this story to touch your heart.*

Write me at:

living_loved@yahoo.com

Made in the USA
Middletown, DE
03 June 2020

96527930R10190